Bible Buddies

Activity Book

for the Old Testament

Bible Skills for Children in Grades 2-3

Developed by Ronnie Smith, Jr.

LifeWay Press
Nashville, Tennessee

Writers
Mikey Thomas Oldham
Mark Swadley
Kaye McKee
Louise Hobson
Fran Hildabrand
Amy Morrow

Nashville, Tennessee
0-7673-3462-0

Dewey Decimal Classification Number: 221.07
Subject Heading: Bible. Old Testament—Study and Teaching
Printed in the United States of America

Children/Preschool Section
Youth/Children/Preschool Department
Discipleship and Family Development Division
The Sunday School Board of the Southern Baptist Convention
127 Ninth Avenue, North
Nashville, Tennessee 37234

Larry Dry, *Section Manager*
Mikey Thomas Oldham, *Design Editor*
Valerie Lynn Smith, *Manuscript Assistant*
Darlene Parrish, *Promotions Editor*
Paula Savage, *Art Director*
Synnöve Inman, *Graphic Designer*

DEAR PARENTS

We are so glad that your child will be attending Bible Buddies. During the next six months we will be learning many things about the Old Testament and also will practice using the Bible in a fun, noncompetitive way.

Bible Buddies is a Bible skills program for children in Grades 2-3. It will prepare your child for Children's Bible Drill, which is for children in Grades 4-6. But even children who do not go on to Bible Drill will gain valuable skills in using and understanding their Bibles.

For example, we will be learning all the books of the Old Testament. In addition, we will learn facts about each book such as the author and some of the important events in the book. A special phrase for each book will help boys and girls remember what each book is about. We will learn the books by divisions or parts of divisions to help children remember them.

The Bible story each week will be one of the Old Testament Key Passages from Children's Bible Drill such as the creation, the Ten Commandments, and Psalm 23. In addition, children will hear stories about major Old Testament Bible people including Moses and David. Some weeks we will have a special feature which will be accounts about how we got our Bible. Other weeks we will have Game Night when we will play games to review everything we have learned.

Children will learn six Old Testament Bible verses. (See the back of this letter. Children will be learning the version that is checked.) These are also verses from Children's Bible Drill. To make learning the verses more fun, children will learn them set to music.

During the meeting each week, we will be playing several games to learn new material and to review. Children also will work two pages in this activity book. They will bring the completed pages home after each meeting. On it will be a Bible reading for them to do the next week. You also will find the phrases for any books they studied.

Our emphasis will be to make this time each week lots of fun as children learn. Each meeting will have at least three to five games.

You can help. Be sure your child is on time since we will be playing a game to teach and review the books of the Bible at the very beginning of each meeting. You can also help by asking your child to review the verses and books being learned each week and by looking over the Bible-reading activity or questions on the activity sheet.

We know your child is going to have a great time learning all about the Old Testament.

In Christ's Name,

Bible Buddies Leaders

BIBLE VERSES TO LEARN

We will be learning the following verses from the King James Version

- **Genesis 1:1**–In the beginning God created the heaven and the earth.
- **Isaiah 45:5**–I am the Lord, and there is none else, there is no God beside me.
- **Numbers 15:39**–Remember all the commandments of the Lord, and do them.
- **Psalm 56:3**–What time I am afraid, I will trust in thee.
- **Isaiah 6:8**–Also I heard the voice of the Lord, saying, Whom shall I send, and who will go for us? Then said I, Here am I; send me.
- **Job 37:14**–Stand still, and consider the wondrous works of God.

We will be learning the following verses from the New International Version

- **Genesis 1:1**–In the beginning God created the heavens and the earth.
- **Isaiah 45:5**–I am the Lord, and there is no other; apart from me there is no God.
- **Numbers 15:39**–Remember all the commands of the Lord, that you may obey them.
- **Psalm 56:3**–When I am afraid, I will trust in you.
- **Isaiah 6:8**–Then I heard the voice of the Lord saying, "Whom shall I send? And who will go for us? And I said, "Here am I. Send me!"
- **Job 37:14**–Stop and consider God's wonders.

Law ◎ History ◎ Poetry ◎ Major Prophets ◎ Minor Prophets

A Special Book

Matching Bible Facts

Your teacher will give you three different colored crayons or markers. Use one to color facts about the Bible. Use another color to color facts about the Old Testament. Use the third color to color facts about the New Testament.

I am made up of two major parts.

I have 39 books.

I am made up of the divisions of Gospels, History, Paul's Letters, General Letters, and Prophecy.

I have 10 divisions.

I tell about Jesus' life.

I have 27 books.

I am inspired by God

I tell about the children of Israel.

I have 66 books.

I come second in the Bible.

I come first in the Bible

I am made up of the divisions of Law, History, Poetry, Major Prophets, and Minor Prophets.

I tell about the early church.

I am divided into the Old Testament and the New Testament.

I tell about creation, Noah, and what happened before the birth of Jesus.

I tell about how God wants people to live.

I tell about the birth of Jesus.

Name Those Divisions

Write the names of the five divisions of the Old Testament on the lines.

1. ___ ___ ___
2. ___ ___ ___ ___ ___ ___ ___
3. ___ ___ ___ ___ ___ ___
4. ___ ___ ___ ___ ___ ___ ___ ___ ___ ___ ___ ___ ___
5. ___ ___ ___ ___ ___ ___ ___ ___ ___ ___ ___ ___ ___

What Does It Spell?

Put the answers to the questions about the Bible story on the lines.
What do the letters in the stars spell?

1. What tells of God's love for all people?
2. One writer was a poet, singer, shepherd, warrior, and king. His name was ________.
3. Paul wrote that the Bible was ____________ or inspired.
4. Some of the books tell the history of the ______________ of israel.
5. Some of the books are written in ________.

1. B ___ ___ ___ ___

2. D ___ ___ ___ ___

3. G ___ ___ - ___ ___ ___ ___ ___ ___ ___ ___

4. C ___ ___ ___ ___ ___ ___ ___

5. P ___ ___ ___ ___ ___

The word spelled in the stars is ___ ___ ___ ___ ___.

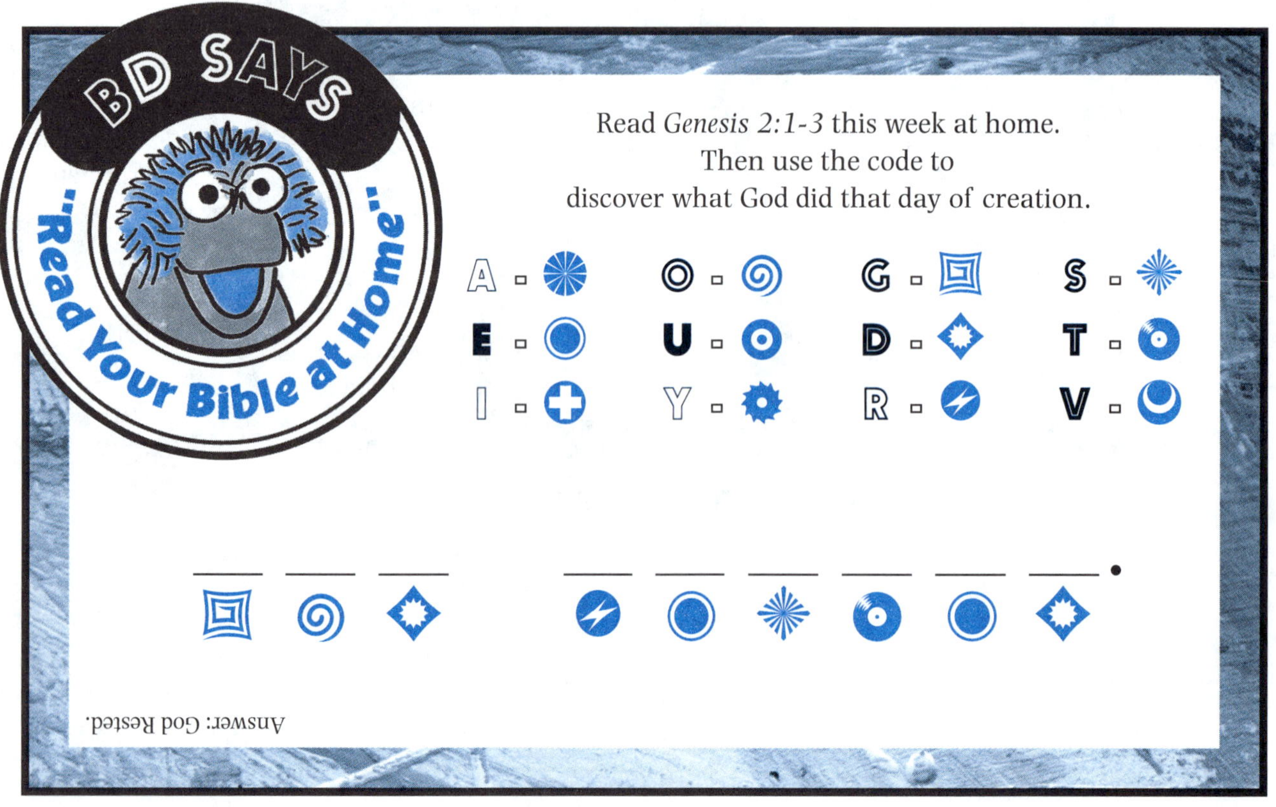

Read *Genesis 2:1-3* this week at home.
Then use the code to
discover what God did that day of creation.

A O G S
E U D T
I Y R V

___ ___ ___ ___ ___ ___ ___ ___ ___.

Answer: God Rested.

The First Seven Days

My Bible Verse

Look at the Bible verse below. Label each part with the correct label: chapter, book, verse.

Find *Genesis 1:1* in your Bibles. Remember that Genesis is the first book in your Bible. Copy the verse in the space below.

Learning the Books of the Bible

This week we are studying the books of Law. It is the first division in the Old Testament. The first five books are called the books of Law. Their names are listed below, but they are scrambled. Write the correct name for each on the line given. Practice saying the names to yourself or to a friend.

issneGe ______________________________

xsoEdu ______________________________

tcivLesui ______________________________

brumeNs ______________________________

eutDreonmyo ______________________________

What Happened When?

Look at the pictures below. Each shape shows what God created on one day.
Match the pictures with the day by drawing a line to each one.
Turn to *Genesis 1* in your Bible for help.

Read the Bible verses some night at home this week.
Then answer the question.

GENESIS 2:15-17

What did God tell man not to do?

The Garden of Eden

My Bible Verse

Write *Genesis 1:1* in the space below. If you need help, use your Bible. Check your verse with your Bible. Tell your neighbor what the verse means.

Learning the Books of the Bible

Below are the five Books of Law. Number them in order. Check your work with your Bible. Practice saying them in order.

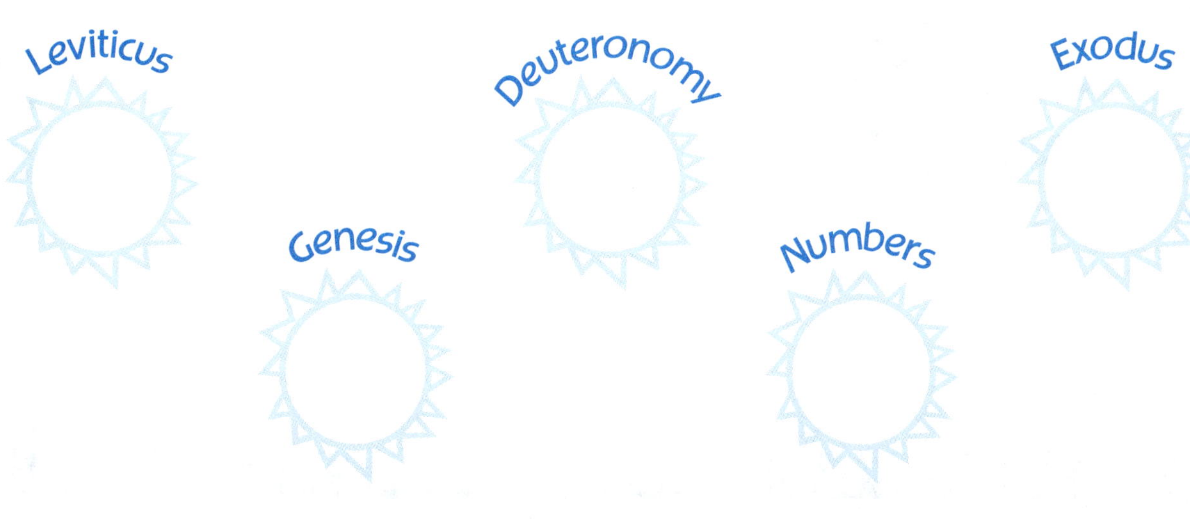

Adam and Eve

Answer the questions about today's Bible story. Then write your answers in the puzzle.

1. God made man from the ____ ____ ____ ____ of the ground. *(Genesis 2:7)*

2. God made all kinds of ____ ____ ____ ____ ____ grow in the first garden. *(Genesis 2:9)*

3. God made woman from man's ____ ____ ____. *(Genesis 2:21)*

4. Man was lonely so God made ____ ____ ____ ____ ____. *(Genesis 2:18, 22)*

5. Man was to take care of the ____ ____ ____ ____ ____ ____. *(Genesis 2:15)*

6. God placed man in the garden of ____ ____ ____ ____. *(Genesis 2:8)*

7. God made the ____ ____ ____ ____ ____ ____ ____ and man named them. *(Genesis 2:19-20)*

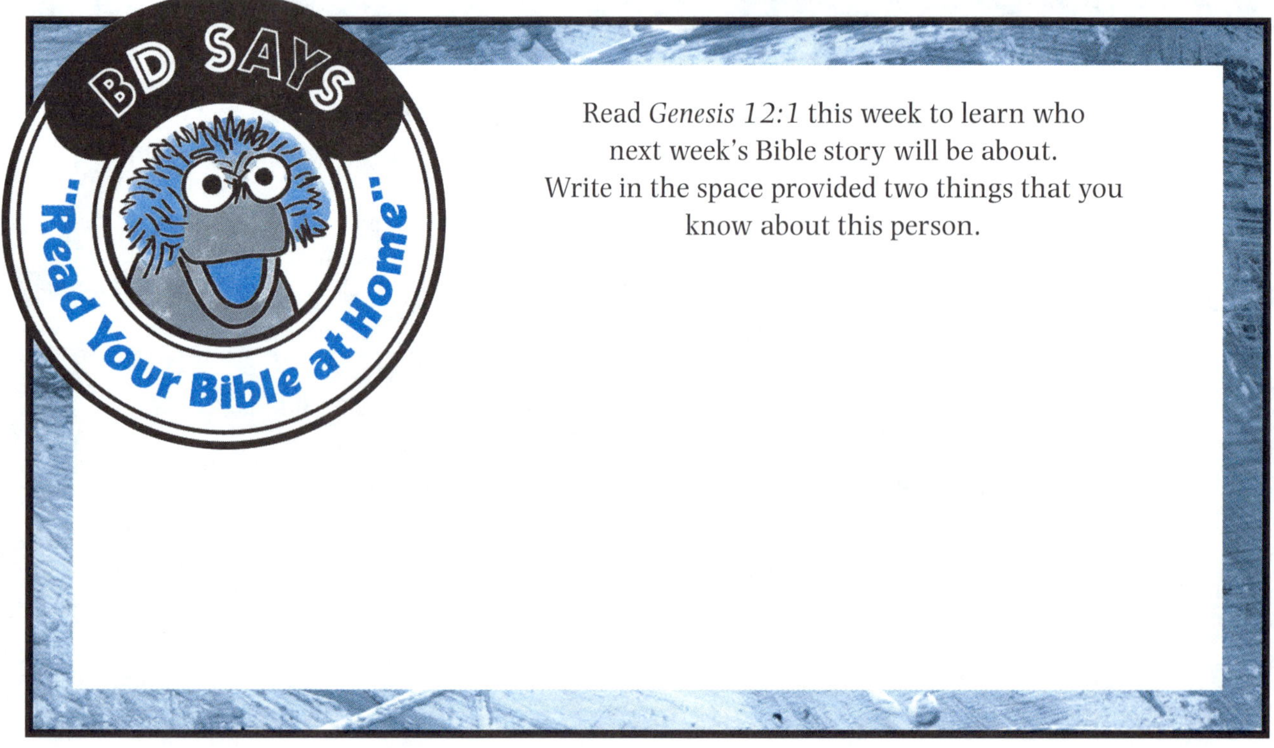

Read *Genesis 12:1* this week to learn who next week's Bible story will be about. Write in the space provided two things that you know about this person.

God Calls Abraham

My Bible Verse

Glue your *Genesis 1:1* card below.
Draw a picture of something God created in the space on the right.

Glue Genesis 1:1 card here.

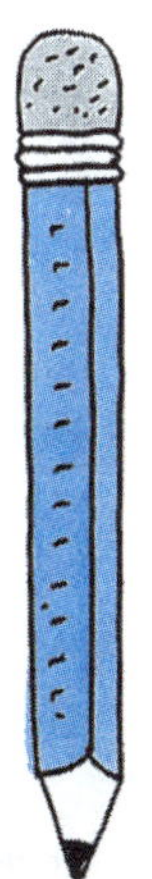

Learning the Books of the Bible

Write the five books of Law on the lines below.
Check your work with your Bible.

God's Covenant with Abraham

Look at the words below. If the words tell something that God promised Abraham, then circle (O) them. If the words are not something God promised, then put an (X) on them.

I will make you famous.

I will place a curse on those who harm you.

I will let you return home in five years.

I will bless those who bless you.

I will give you a big house.

I will bless you.

I will make you king.

I will make you a great nation.

I will give you anything you want.

All the people on earth will be blessed because of you.

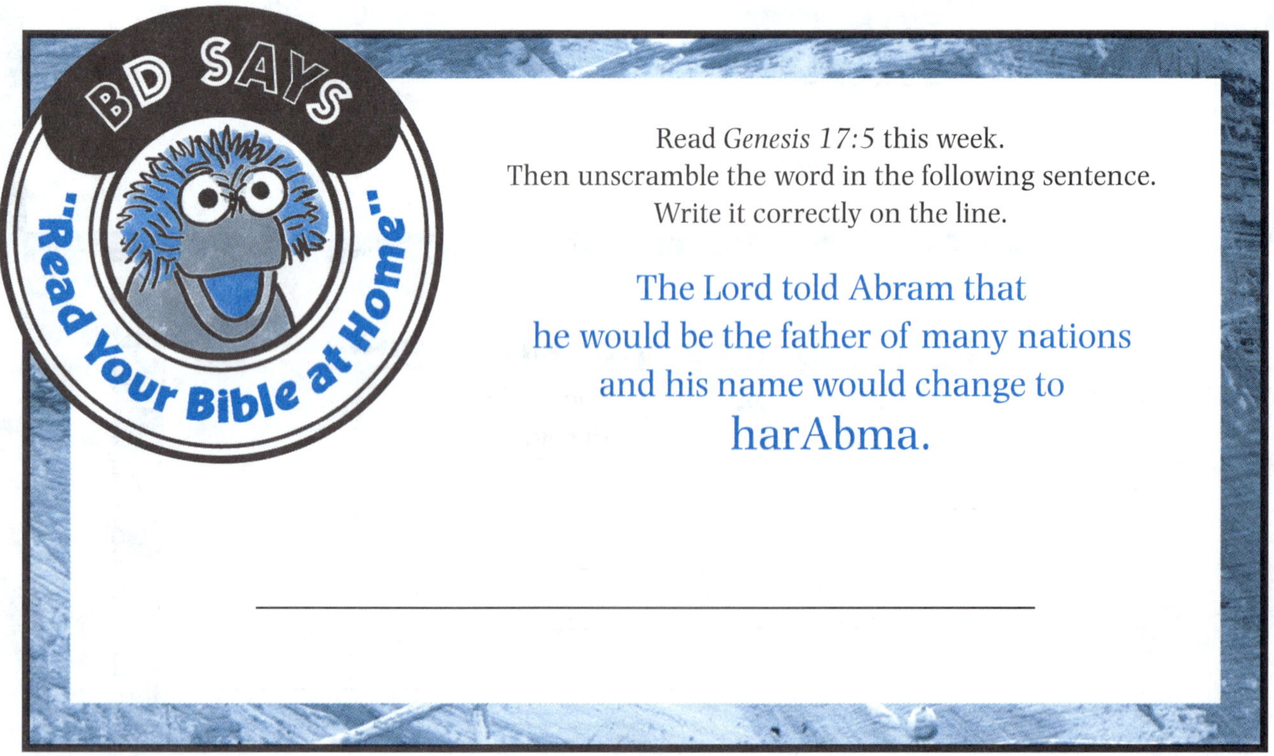

Read *Genesis 17:5* this week.
Then unscramble the word in the following sentence.
Write it correctly on the line.

The Lord told Abram that he would be the father of many nations and his name would change to harAbma.

____

Abraham's Life

Put Abraham's Life in Order

Below are four scenes from Abraham's life. Under the correct picture write the words from the title box. Then place the scenes in order by placing a number in the picture corner.

Title Box	
1. Abraham prays for others.	**3.** Abraham offers Isaac to God.
2. Abraham cares for three visitors.	**4.** Abraham lets Lot choose first.

______________________________ ______________________________

______________________________ ______________________________

Find the Law Books

Circle (○) the book of Law in each group. Then write the books of Law in order.

(Amos ◎ Isaiah ◎ Exodus)

(Ecclesiastes ◎ Esther ◎ Deuteronomy)

(1 Chronicles ◎ Leviticus ◎ Job)

(Judges ◎ Genesis ◎ Psalms)

(Numbers ◎ Ezra ◎ Joshua)

1. ______________________________
2. ______________________________
3. ______________________________
4. ______________________________
5. ______________________________

Which Book is It?

Check the book of Law that is described in the scroll.

God is Holy

- ◎ Genesis
- ◎ Leviticus
- ◎ Exodus
- ◎ Numbers
- ◎ Deuteronomy

Chosen by God

- ◎ Genesis
- ◎ Leviticus
- ◎ Exodus
- ◎ Numbers
- ◎ Deuteronomy

In the Beginning

- ◎ Genesis
- ◎ Leviticus
- ◎ Exodus
- ◎ Numbers
- ◎ Deuteronomy

In the Wilderness

- ◎ Genesis
- ◎ Leviticus
- ◎ Exodus
- ◎ Numbers
- ◎ Deuteronomy

Exit and Journey

- ◎ Genesis
- ◎ Leviticus
- ◎ Exodus
- ◎ Numbers
- ◎ Deuteronomy

Psalm 119 is the longest book in the Bible. It is full of good advice about reading, studying, and obeying God's Word. Read the verses at home this week and match them to their meaning. Check your answers using the answer key at the bottom of the page.

_____ **1.** *Psalm 119:1*

_____ **2.** *Psalm 119:73*

_____ **3.** *Psalm 119:97*

_____ **4.** *Psalm 119:105*

A. God's word is a lamp to our feet and a light for our path.

B. God made us and gives us understanding to learn His commands.

C. God blesses those who walk by His laws.

D. Those who love God's law think about it all day.

Answer Key: 1c, 2b, 3d, 4a

Joshua: Conquering the Land © Judges: Being Disobedient

Bible History

Discover Joshua and Judges

Use the Hebrew code to fill in the blanks.
As you decode, you will find important facts about Joshua and Judges.

JOSHUA	JUDGES
fiרסת בook of הiסתoרy	סeשoנד בook of הiסתoרy
שoנqueרiנג תהe לaנד	בeiנג דiסoבeדieנת
רaהaב aנד תהe סpieס	גoד puנiסהiנג תהe סoנס of Iסרaeל
תהe faלל of Jeרiשהo	גoד רaiסeד up שהampioנס

The One and Only God

Look up the words of *Isaiah 45:5* in your Bible and copy the verse in the scroll.
Say the verse to a friend.

A Bible Recipe

How the Bible Came to Us

God could have given us the Bible without any help from human beings, but He chose to use people to put together His inspired Word. Circle (○) the things that were used to put together the Bible. Cross out the things that were not needed to produce the first Bibles.

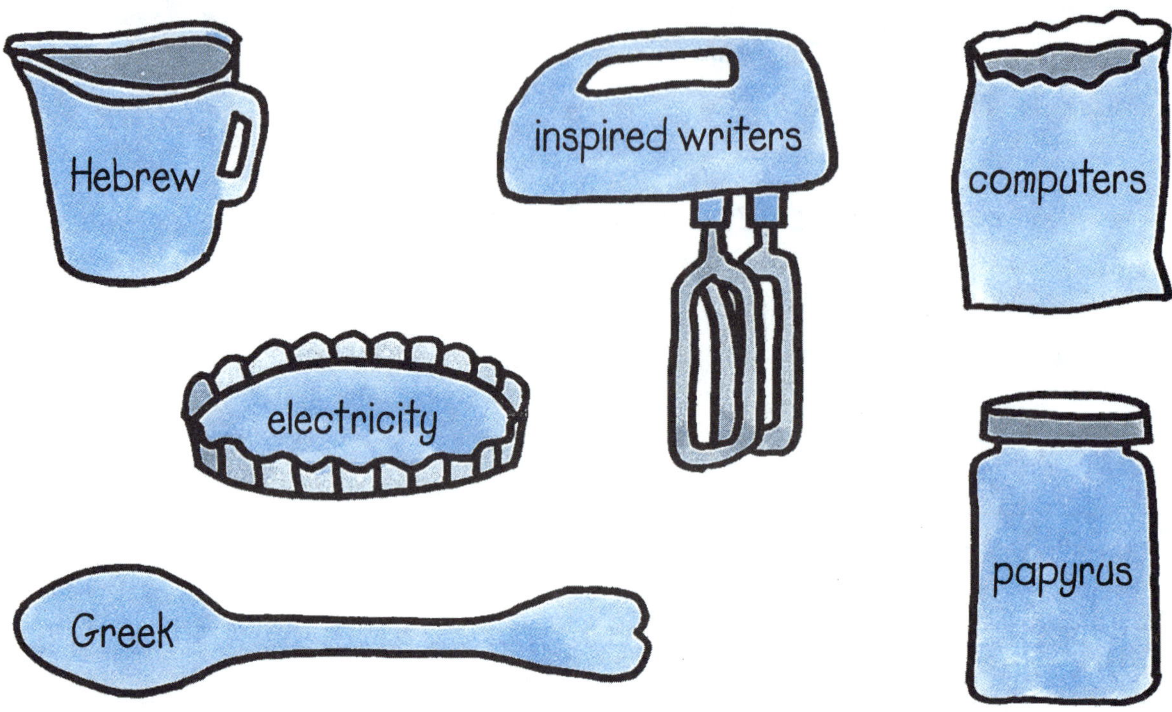

BD SAYS "Read Your Bible at Home"

Joshua stood strong for God. Read *Joshua 1:6-9*. Write the passage in your own words or by using phrases from the idea box.

____

____

____

____

____

____

Idea Box

Be strong
Have courage
Obey God's law
Read the Bible
Follow God to succeed
God is with you

meeting 7

Ruth: Faithful to Family ◎ 1 Samuel: The Kings ◎ 2 Samuel: Life of David

Bible Book Activities

Books of History Jumble

Unscramble the 12 books of History. Use your Bible to check your answers.

ahuJso	J							gni2sK	2	K								
gedsuJ	J							les1noricCh	1	C								
tRuh	R							roniChcles2	2	C								
muleSa1	1	S						zEar	E									
lea2mSu	2	S						heemiNah	N									
gni2sK	1	K						herstE	E									

Build the Walls to Find the Book Phrase

Copy the letters from the matching shapes onto the walls to discover the Bible book phrases.

RUTH ________________________________

1 SAMUEL ________________________________

2 SAMUEL ________________________________

Books of Law and History Maze

Work your way through this maze to find the books of Law and the books of History in order. Read them to a friend.

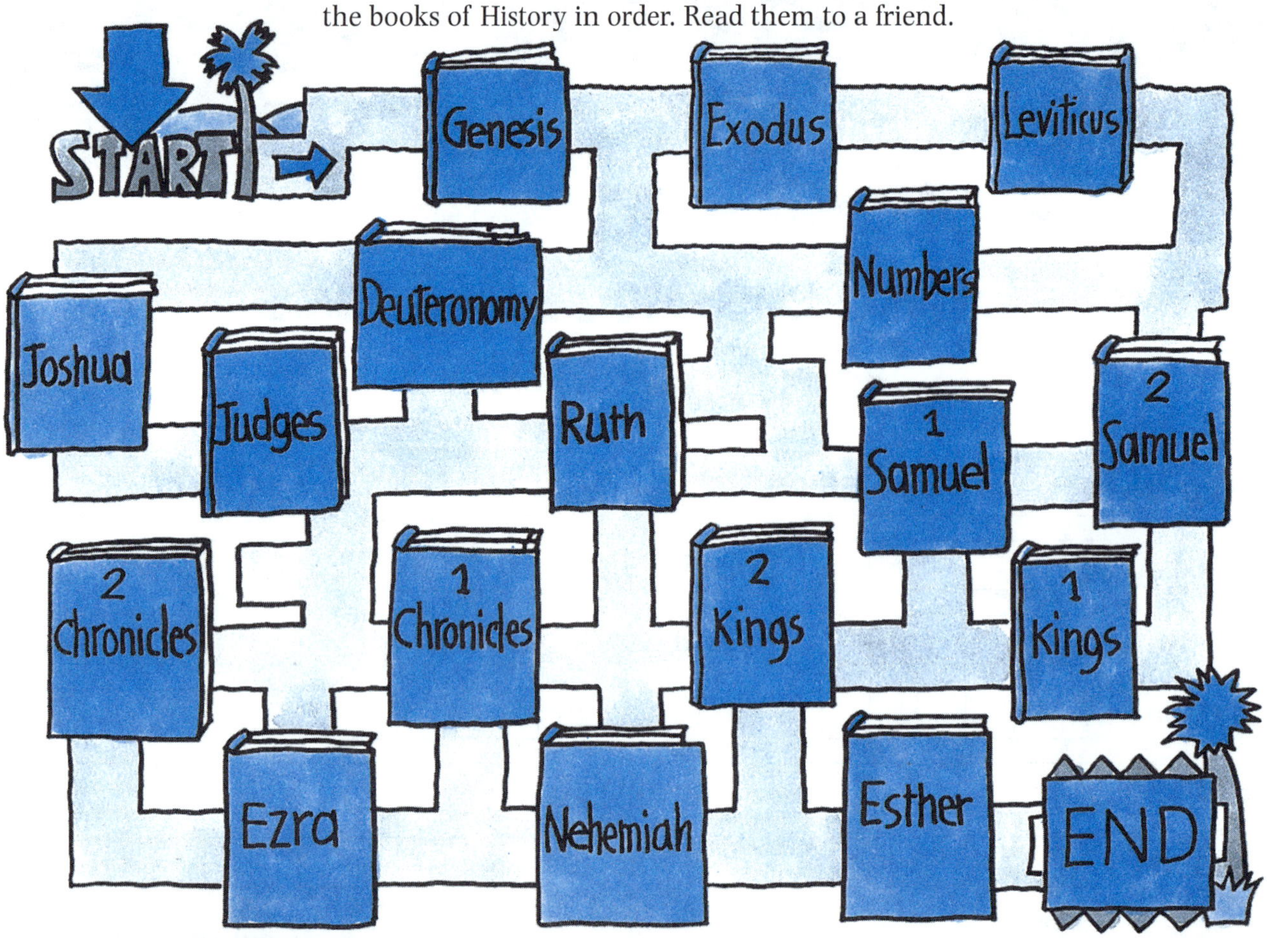

START
Genesis
Exodus
Leviticus
Numbers
Deuteronomy
Joshua
Judges
Ruth
1 Samuel
2 Samuel
1 Kings
2 Kings
1 Chronicles
2 Chronicles
Ezra
Nehemiah
Esther
END

BD SAYS
"Read Your Bible at Home"

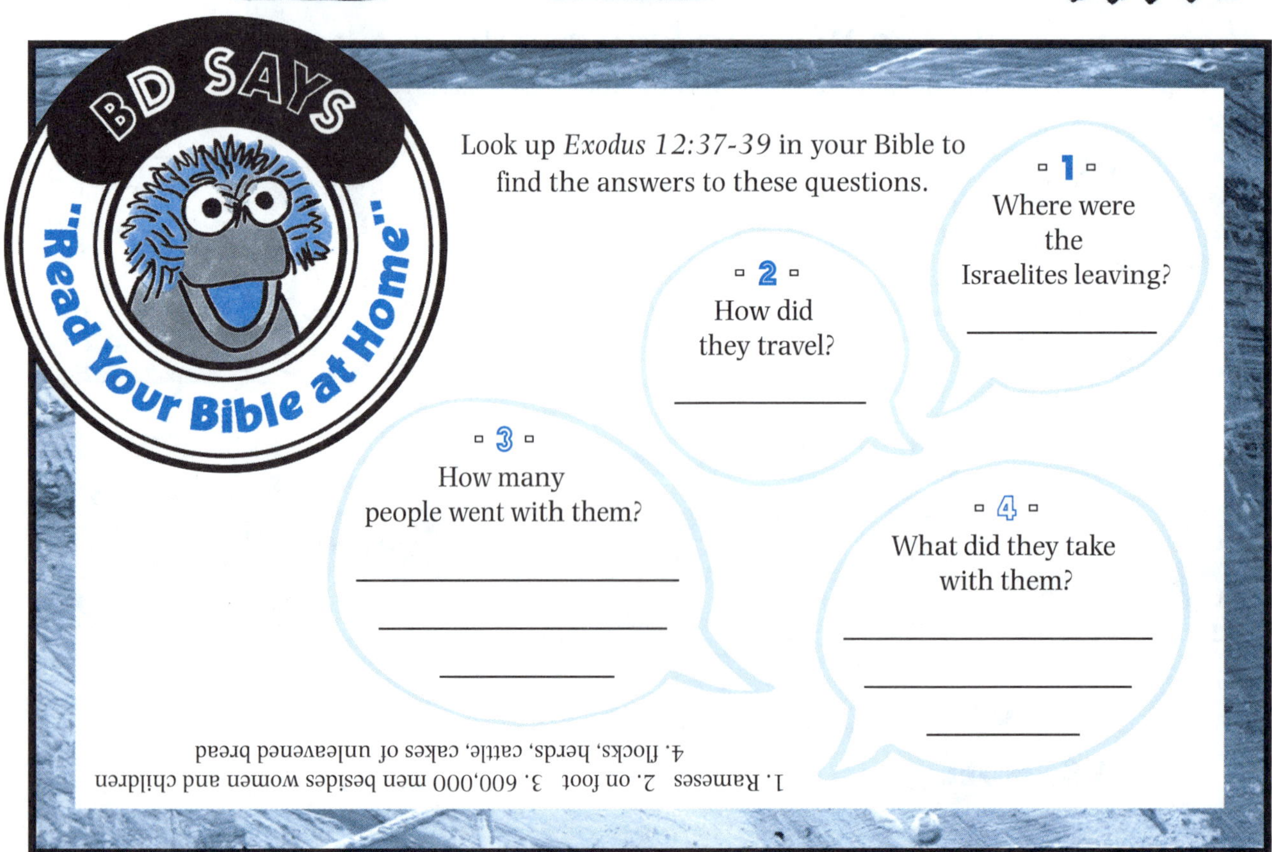

Look up *Exodus 12:37-39* in your Bible to find the answers to these questions.

1. Where were the Israelites leaving? ______________

2. How did they travel? ______________

3. How many people went with them? ______________ ______________ ______________

4. What did they take with them? ______________ ______________ ______________

1. Rameses 2. on foot 3. 600,000 men besides women and children
4. flocks, herds, cattle, cakes of unleavened bread

1 Kings: Solomon the Wise ◎ 2 Kings: Exile to Babylon ◎ 1 Chronicles: David Again ◎ 2 Chronicles: Solomon Again

The Israelites Leave Egypt

Match the Book and Phrase

Draw lines between the name of the Bible book and the phrase that goes with the book.

What Was Taken From Egypt?

Follow the footprints to find the items that the Bible tells us the Israelites took with them when they left Egypt. Cross out (X) the footprints of the items that were not taken out of Egypt. Look up *Exodus 12:31-42* to check your answer.

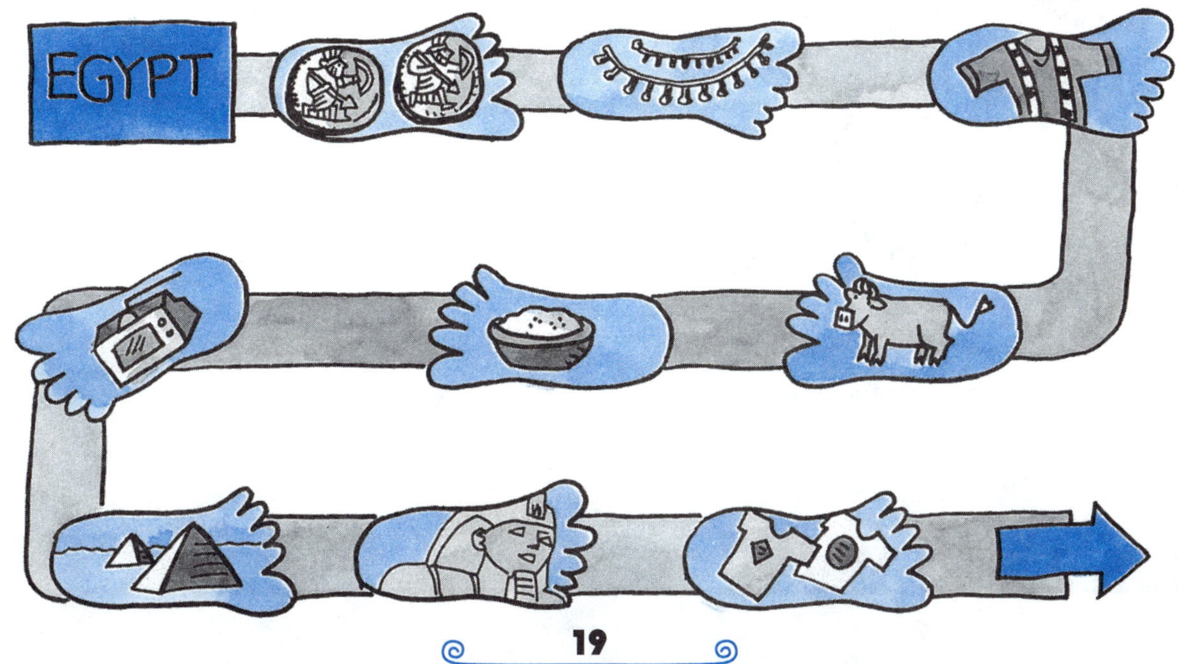

A Puzzling Puzzle

Can you work a crossword puzzle with no clues?

The books of Law and History are in the puzzle. Use the first letters to fill in each one.

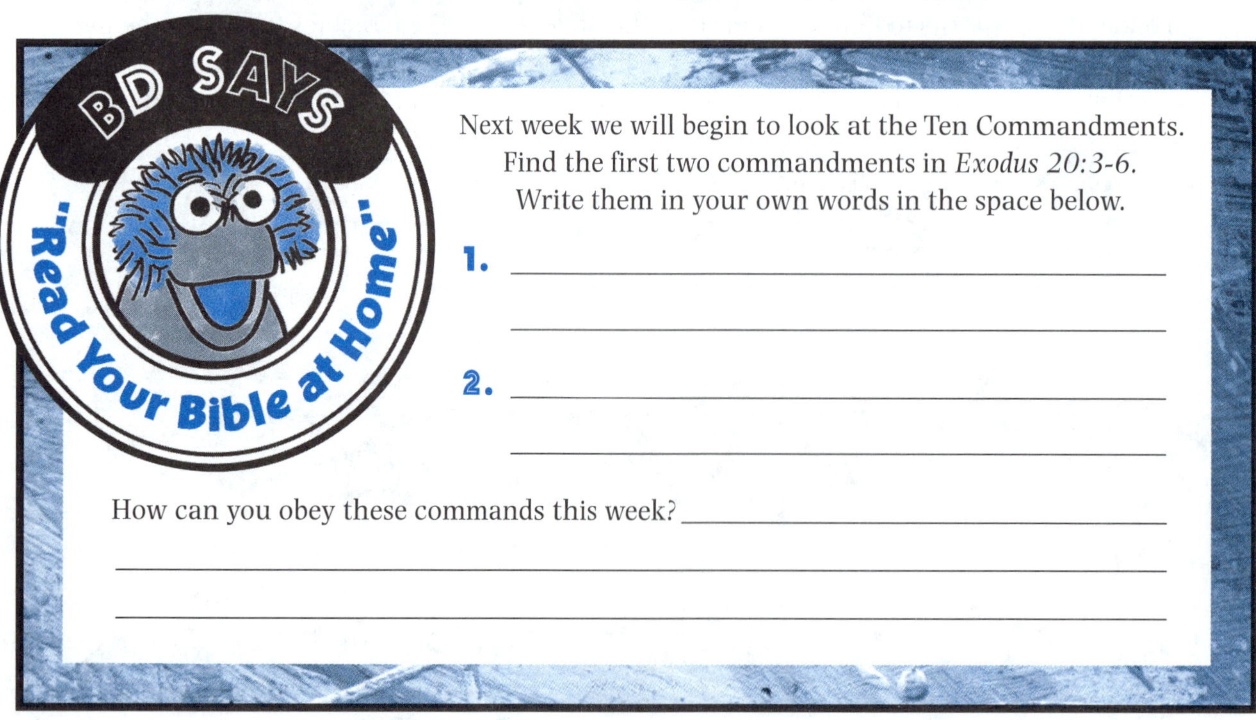

Next week we will begin to look at the Ten Commandments. Find the first two commandments in *Exodus 20:3-6*. Write them in your own words in the space below.

1. ______________________________

____

2. ______________________________

____

How can you obey these commands this week? ______________________________

____

____

Ezra: Rebuild the Temple ◎ Nehemiah: Rebuild the Walls ◎ Esther: The Queen

God and Me

Bible Fact Find

Color in the corresponding numbered Bible for each correct statement.
Draw a line through each incorrect statement.

1. God gave us rules for living.
2. Everything will be fine if we do whatever we feel like doing.
3. We find 10 rules for living in the Book of Genesis.
4. Exodus 20 records the Ten Commandments.
5. The first four commandments teach us how to be good friends with God.
6. God wants us to worship only Him.
7. God wants us to rest and think about Him.

History in Living Color

Color the two words that describe Ezra–*yellow*.
Color the two words about Nehemiah–*red*. Color the two words about Esther–*blue*.
Then below the word box, show how you can be like one of these Bible history persons.

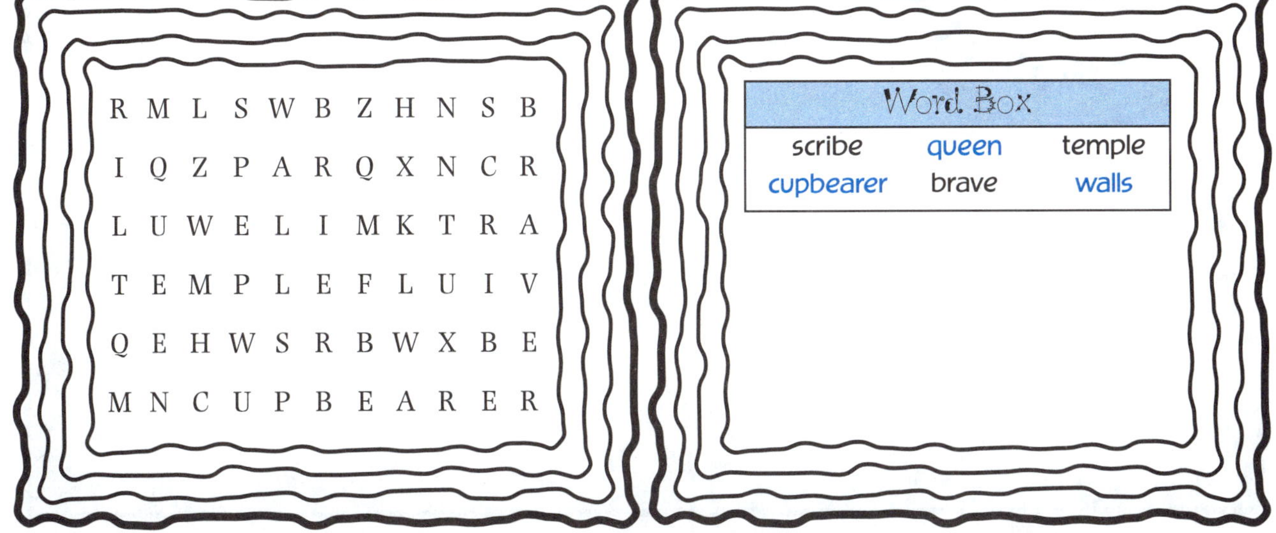

No Other God

In your Bible find and read *Isaiah 45:5.*

Draw an (X) through things boys and girls can make more important than God.

Putting God first is always the best choice!

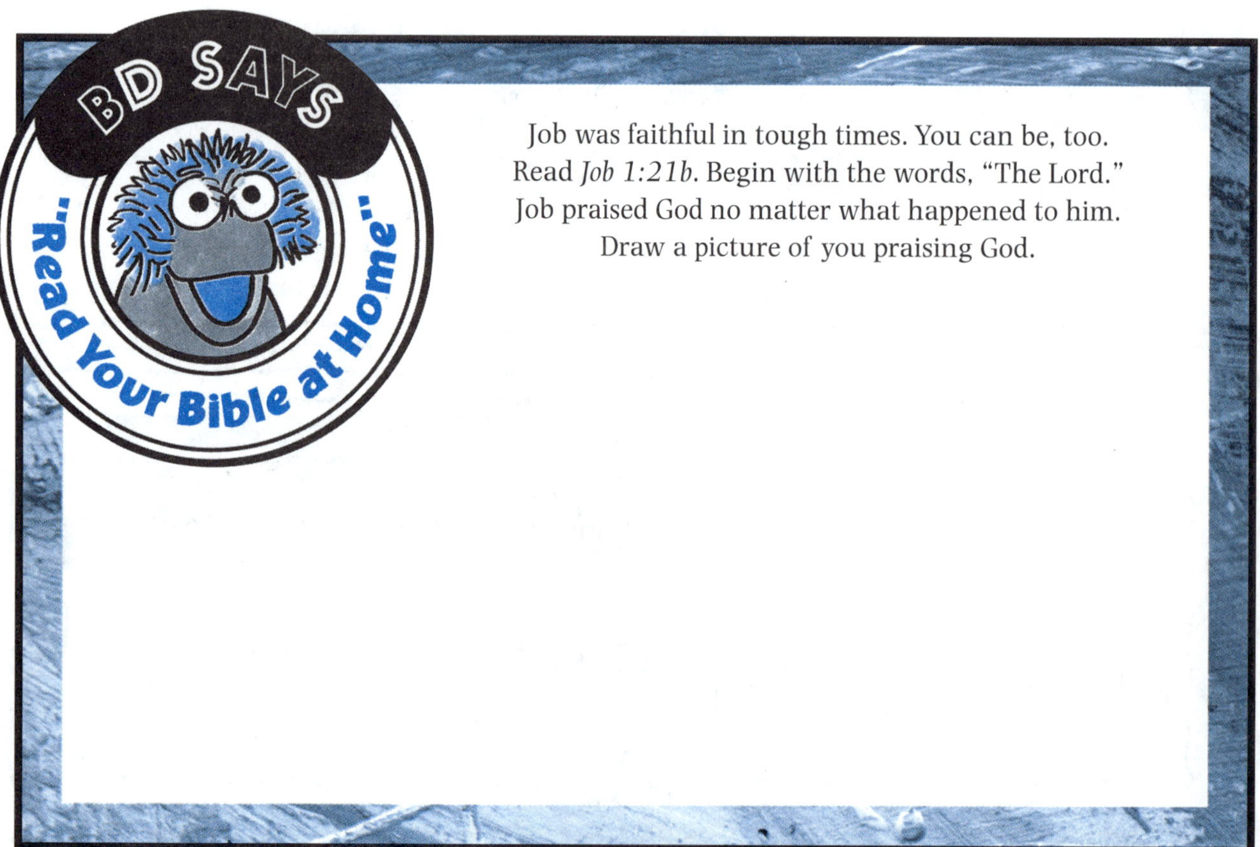

Job was faithful in tough times. You can be, too. Read *Job 1:21b*. Begin with the words, "The Lord." Job praised God no matter what happened to him. Draw a picture of you praising God.

Job: Suffering ◎ Job: Suffering ◎ Job: Suffering ◎ Job: Suffering ◎ Job: Suffering ◎ Job: Suffering

A Good Neighbor

Being a Good Neighbor

Can you be a good neighbor? Of course! God has shown you how. Draw a line to match each command to a way you can obey it.

Dear Lord, help me to keep my wedding promises always.

I really want this game, but I'll wait until I can buy it.

▫ 5 ▫ Obey your parents.

▫ 6 ▫ Do not murder.

▫ 7 ▫ Keep your wedding promises.

▫ 8 ▫ Do not steal.

▫ 9 ▫ Do not lie.

▫ 10 ▫ Do not want what others have.

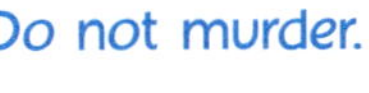

I'm not going to hurt my body or anyone else's.

When I listen, Dad teaches me about God.

Mrs. Strickland, I'm the one who cheated, not Angela.

I wish I had shoes like that, but I'm glad Ted has them.

Learning from Job

Job learned from his tough times. You can, too. Read the statements and fill in the blanks. Use the word in the shaded circles in a sentence about Job.

1. Job had ________ sons and three daughters. *(Job 1:2)*
2. Job was from the land of ________________. *(Job 1:1)*
3. Even though Job lost much, he ________________ to the ground and worshiped God. *(Job 1:20)*
4. Job got sores all over from his ________________ to his head. *(Job 2:7)*
5. Job's _______ told him to curse God and die. *(Job 2:9)*
6. Three __________ came to give Job advice. *(Job 2:11)*

1. ◯ ___ V ___ ___
2. ◯ Z
3. ◯ E ___ ___
4. ◯ ___ ___ T
5. W ___ ___ ◯
6. ___ ◯ ___ E ___ D ___

Not even having to ________________ caused Job to curse God.

Scope It Out

Get out your magnifying glass and study *Numbers 15:39*.

The verse tells you to __________ the Lord's __________ and __________ them.

Read *Psalm 139:1-4*. In the wedges draw some of the things God knows about you.

The Life of Moses

Traveling Through Moses' Life

Remember traveling through Moses' life in the Bible-story time?
Number the events in the order in which they occurred.

Math Code

Use your math skills to learn Bible skills!

How many books are in the Law division? $10 - 8 =$ ______ $+ 3 =$ ______

How many books come before Deuteronomy? $5 + 3 =$ ______ $- 4 =$ ______

How many Old Testament books are pairs *(like first and second)* $1 + 1 =$ ______ $+ 1 =$ ______

How many books are in the Poetry division? $6 - 5 =$ ______ $+ 4 =$ ______

What Law book has to do with math? ________________________________

Memory Power

Knowing God's commands gives you power for living.

Read *Numbers 15:39*. What can you do to remember the Lord's commands?

1. ________________________________

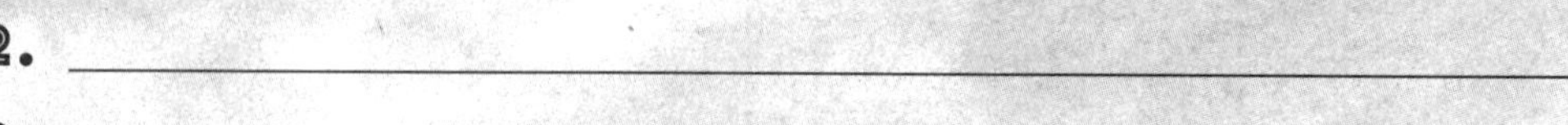

2. ________________________________

3. ________________________________

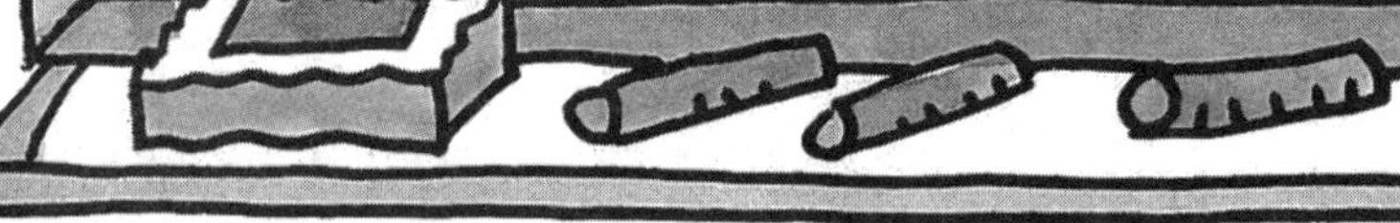

You will love this passage! Read *Ecclesiastes 3:1-5*.
On the calendar list the times which you look forward to.

CALENDAR

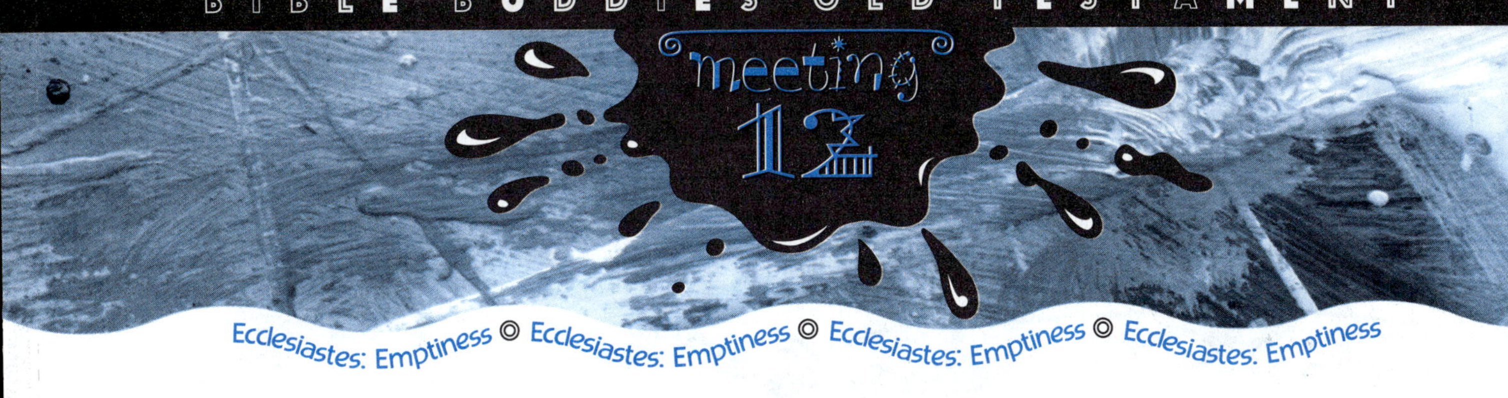

Bible History

Breaking the Code

Hey, everybody, I have something to tell you! I lkthlii liwkcuie jdiu leiyw g wjmlck! Can you believe it? What did all that mean? Well, that is just how people feel when they try to read a language they do not understand. Imagine how the Jews from Alexandria felt about reading the Old Testament in the Hebrew language. Bible translators do important work! Be a Bible translator. Use the code below the review what we learned today.

Most people in Bible times hired S C R ___ B ___ S to do their writing.

Bible-time scribes wore L ___ N ___ N clothing.

The prophet J __ R __ M __ __ H told his scribe Baruch to write what he said.

S __ V __ N T __ - T __ __ Jewish scholars translated the Old Testament into G R __ __ K.

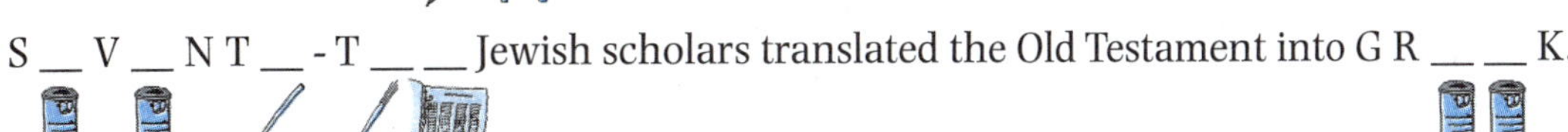

The Greek Old Testament translation is called the S __ P T __ __ G __ N T, which means S __ V __ N T __.

Flying High

Draw a string to connect each poetry book to its main idea.

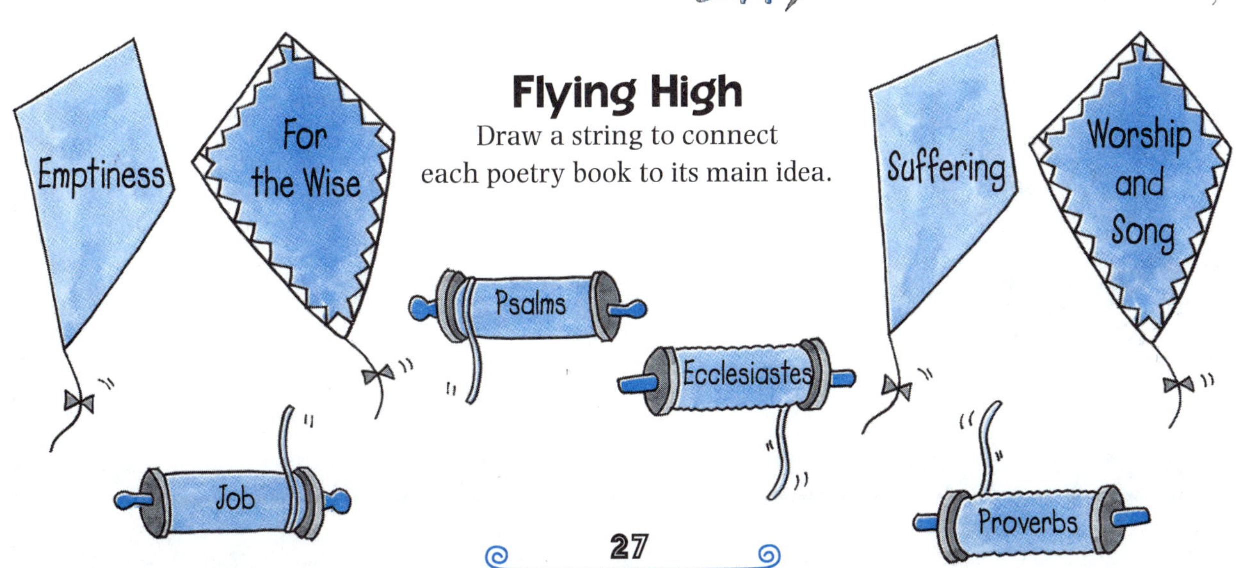

Monkwriting

Monk scribes ran their words together with no spaces between. Like this

IAMABIBLEBUDDY

Using monkstyle writing, print your idea of what *Numbers 15:39* means.
See if someone in your family can read what you wrote.

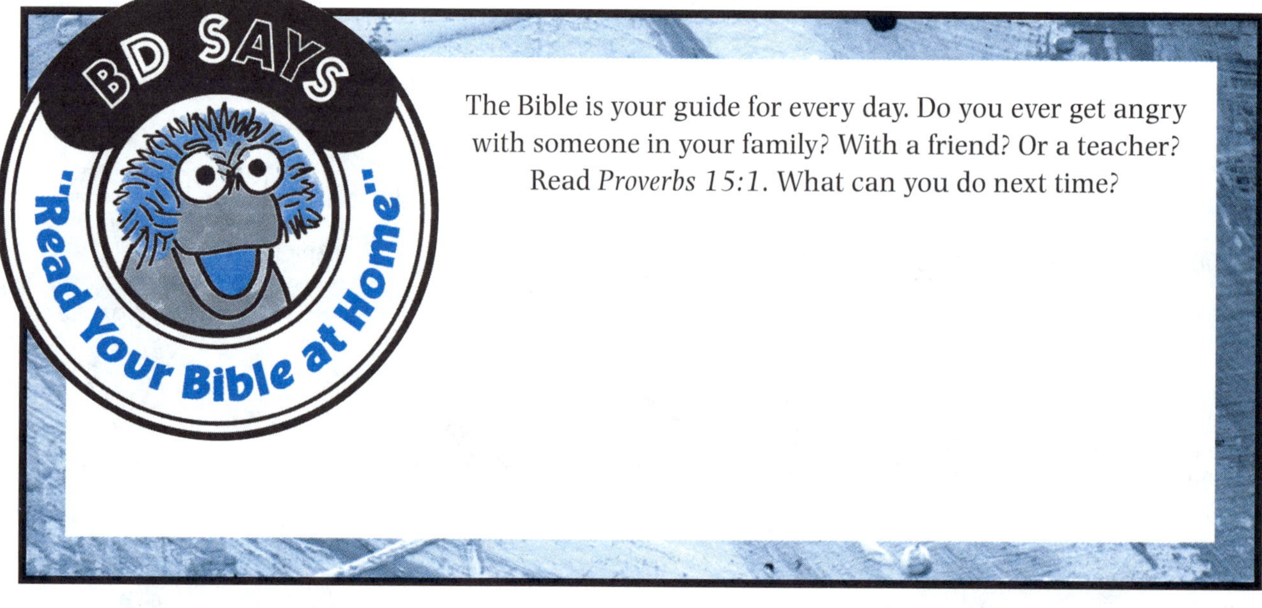

The Bible is your guide for every day. Do you ever get angry with someone in your family? With a friend? Or a teacher? Read *Proverbs 15:1*. What can you do next time?

Song of Solomon (Song of Songs)

Love Check

Sure, Song of Solomon, or Song of Songs, is a book of love songs. Sure, it sounds awfully mushy. But you have probably thought about getting married someday. Let's think God's way. Check some things you can do now to make yourself God's kind of wife or husband. You might not get married at all and that is OK. Circle (○) things that would make you the kind of person God wants you to be—and, after all, that is the most important thing.

Read my Bible regularly.

Pray for the person I will marry. (Yes, even though you won't marry for a long time!)

Think about what other people need.

Find ways to show others I love them.

There is lots more to getting married than picking out flowers. Marriage is SERIOUS business. It is never too early to start thinking of the kind of person you might marry!

Remember God's Commands and Do Them

Read *Numbers 15:39*. Place an (X) below each statement that is one of God's commands. Circle (○) each one you intend to keep this week.

Do God's Commands ◎ Do God's commands

Obey your parents.

____

Do not steal.

____

Remember the Sabbath day by keeping it holy.

____

Do not have any other gods before Me.

____

Do God's commands ◎ Do God's Commands

Link the Books

Look at the book names below. Use a *red* crayon to connect the books of Law in order. Use a *green* crayon to connect the books of History in order. Use a *blue* crayon to connect the books of Poetry in order.

Genesis
Joshua
2 Chronicles
Ezra
Judges
Psalms
Exodus
2 Samuel
1 Kings
Song of Solomon (Songs)
Proverbs
2 Kings
1 Chronicles
1 Samuel
Nehemiah
Leviticus
Ecclesiastes
Esther
Numbers
Ruth
Deuteronomy
Job

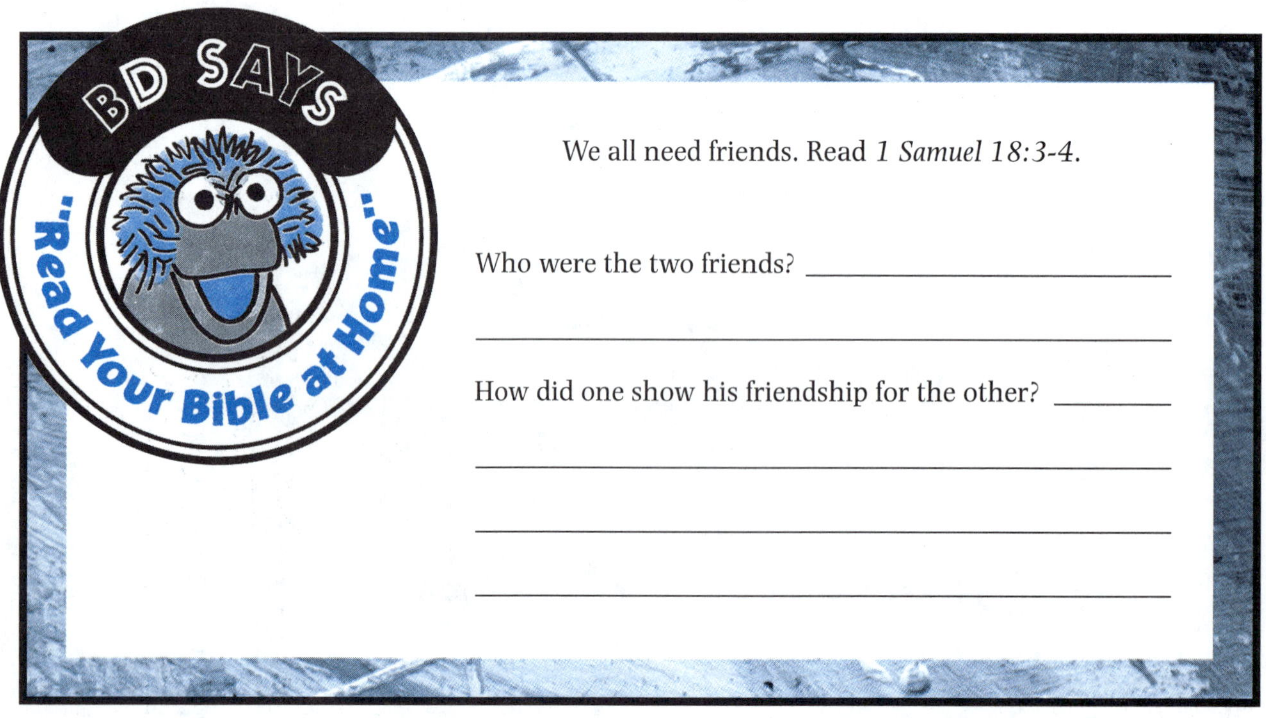

We all need friends. Read *1 Samuel 18:3-4*.

Who were the two friends? ______________________

____

How did one show his friendship for the other? ________

____

____

____

The Life of David

Fill In the Letters

Discover the titles of the five books of the Major Prophets division. These books are found in the Old Testament. Use the code to help you fill in the missing letters.

To help you remember the names of the Bible books, you will learn a phrase. This phrase tells you what each book is about. The sentence below the books tells about the Book of Isaiah.

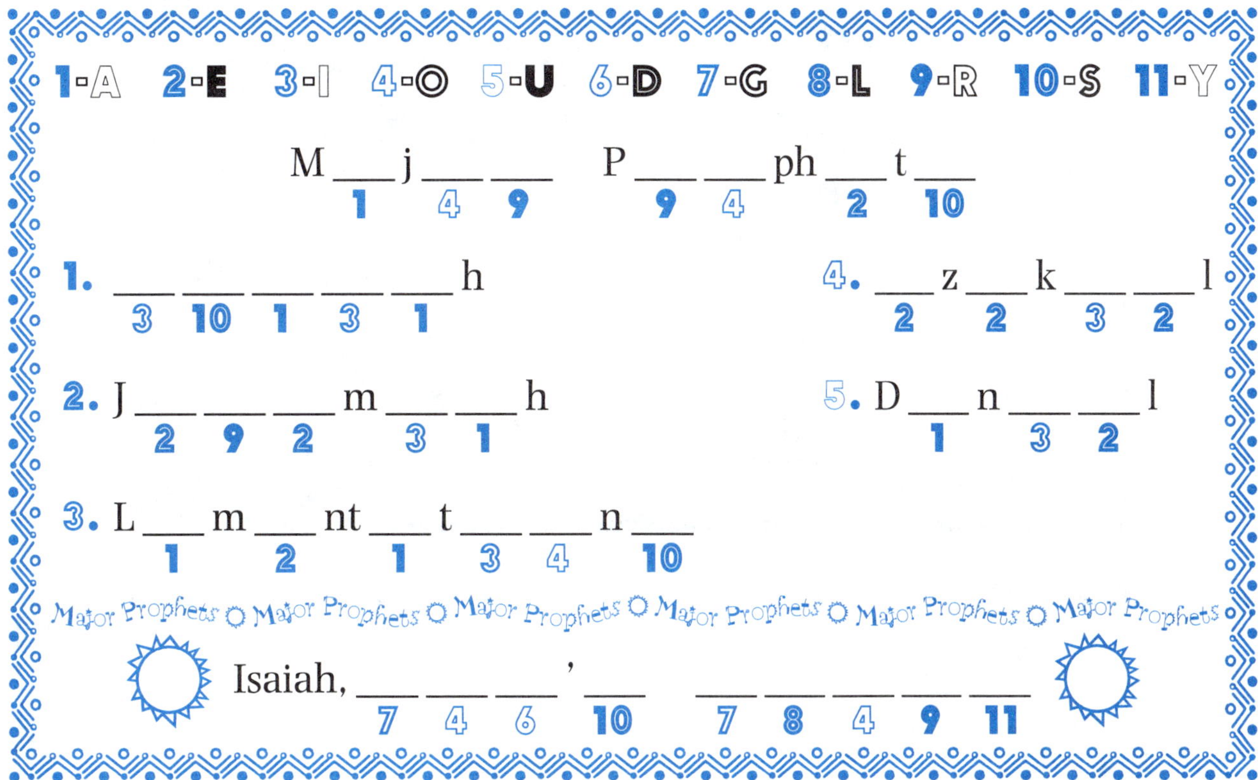

Psalm 56:3 and You

Find and read *Psalm 56:3* in your Bible.
Think about the verse. Then in the blanks below write times when you might be afraid.

◎ When I am afraid of ______________________________, I will trust in You, God.

◎ When I am afraid of ______________________________, I will trust in You, God.

◎ When I am afraid of ______________________________, I will trust in You, God.

Puzzling about David

Use the words in the word box to help you complete the crossword puzzle about David.

1. David was a *(2 down)* boy, taking care of his father's sheep.
2. David wrote *(2 across)* and *(5 across)*.
3. David used a *(3 down)* and *(4 across)* to kill the giant, *(6 across)*.
4. David served as a *(4 down)* in King Saul's army.
5. David played a *(7 across)* for King Saul.
6. God chose David to be the second *(1 down)* of Israel.

Word Box	
Goliath	harp
poems	soldier
songs	stones
king	slingshot
shepherd	

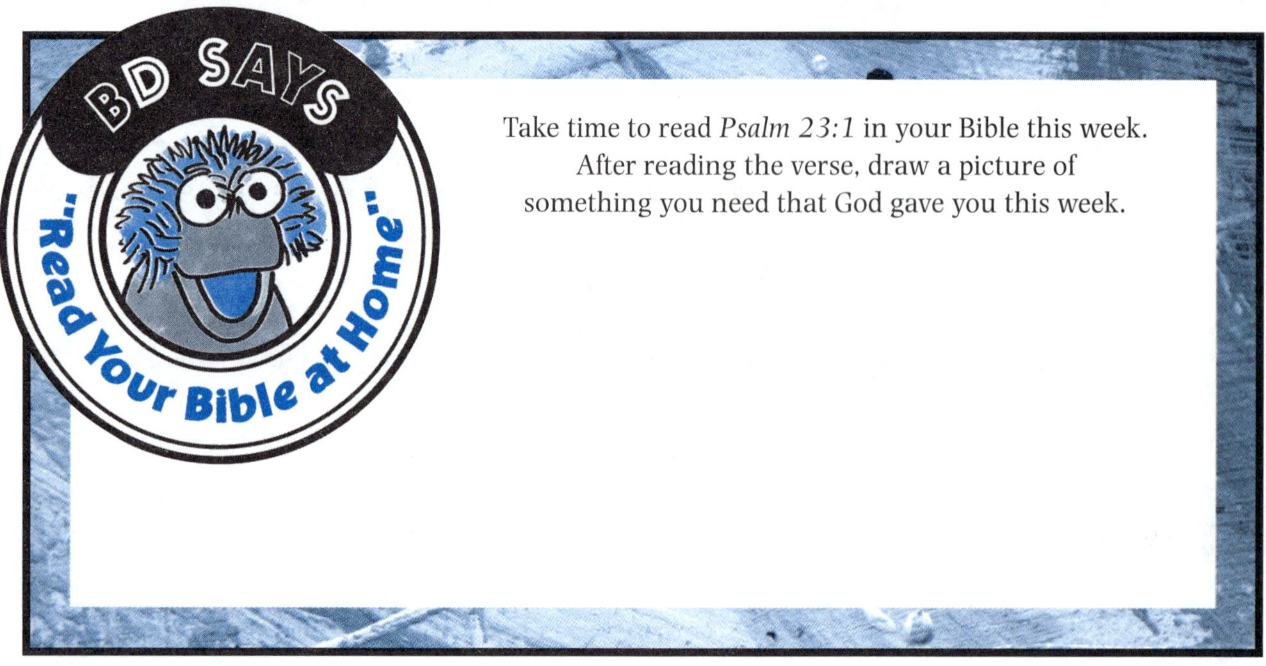

Take time to read *Psalm 23:1* in your Bible this week. After reading the verse, draw a picture of something you need that God gave you this week.

Jeremiah: A Nation in Ruin ◎ Lamentations: A Time to Cry

A Shepherd's Song: Psalm 23

Bible Division Book Review

On the line under each book title, write the Old Testament division to which it belongs.
Give yourself 10 points for each one you fill in correctly from memory.
Give yourself 5 points for each one you fill in by looking at the Bible chart in the room.

Exodus	Nehemiah	Proverbs	Isaiah	
______ points	______ points	______ points	______ points	______
Lamentations	Esther	Judges	Psalms	
______ points	______ points	______ points	______ points	______
Leviticus	Ruth	Job	Jeremiah	
______ points	______ points	______ points	______ points	______

Total Points ______

Trusting God

Circle the pictures that show something that would cause you to be afraid.

Find and read *Psalm 56:3* in your Bible.
Write the Bible verse in the space below.

Who will you trust when you are afraid? ______________________

Psalm 23

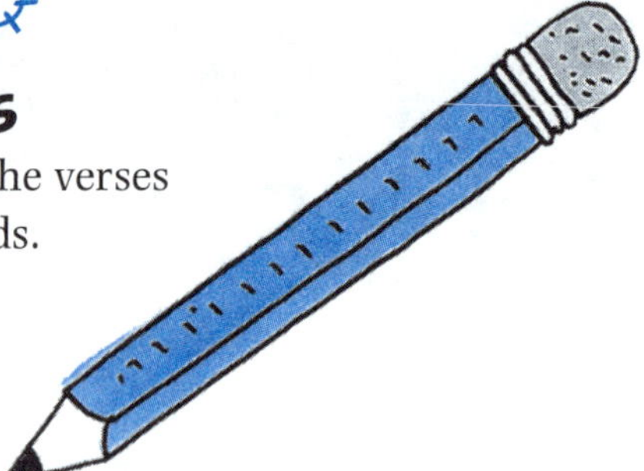

Find the Answers

Open your Bible to *Psalm 23.* Read the verses and write in the missing words.

1. David said the Lord was his ____________________________. *(v. 1)*
2. David said the shepherd would make him lie down in __________________. *(v. 2)*
3. David said the shepherd would lead or guide him in paths of ______________. *(v. 3)*
4. David said he would fear no ____________________________. *(v. 4)*
5. David said he would not be afraid because ________________ are with him. *(v. 4)*
6. David believed ______________ and ______________ follow him all his life. *(v. 6)*
7. David felt sure he would live in ________________________ forever. *(v. 6)*

This week be sure to read *Psalm 51:6* and *Psalm 51:12* in your Bible. Unscramble the words below.

In these two verses the writer asks God for

swimod ________________________

and yjo ________________.

meeting 16

Ezekiel: Promise to Restore ◎ Ezekiel: Promise to Restore ◎ Ezekiel: Promise to Restore

A Prayer for Forgiveness–Psalm 51

Ezekiel Matching Activity

Draw a line from column 1 to column 2 to complete the sentences.

Column 1	Column 2
Ezekiel was a ◎	◎ broken down.
Ezekiel told the people ◎	◎ hope.
Ezekiel told God's message when he was a ◎	◎ priest and prophet.
Ezekiel told about when the walls of Jerusalem were ◎	◎ restored.
But Ezekiel also brought God's message of ◎	◎ captive.
He told the people that Israel would be ◎	◎ Jerusalem would fall.

Bible Books Math

Open your Bible to the contents page. Work the Bible book math: find the name of the book given. Count forward for +. Count backwards for -. Place the word answer in the block over the Bible book name you found. The first problem is worked for you.

Problems

Genesis + 4 =	Deuteronomy	= to		Ruth − 7 =	________	= When
Esther + 2 =	________	= I		2 Kings + 11 =	________	= am
Lamentations + 2 =	________	= must		Proverbs + 4 =	________	= I
Daniel − 1 =	________	= trust		Job + 7 =	________	= afraid
Isaiah − 3 =	________	= God		Numbers + 2 =	________	= remember

________	________	________	________	________
Genesis	Jeremiah	Isaiah	Lamentations	Psalms
________	________	to	________	________
Daniel	Joshua	Deuteronomy	Exekiel	Proverbs

What message is given?

____

Number the Books

Number the books in order by placing the number of each book on the lines below. Check your work with the Table of Contents in your Bible.

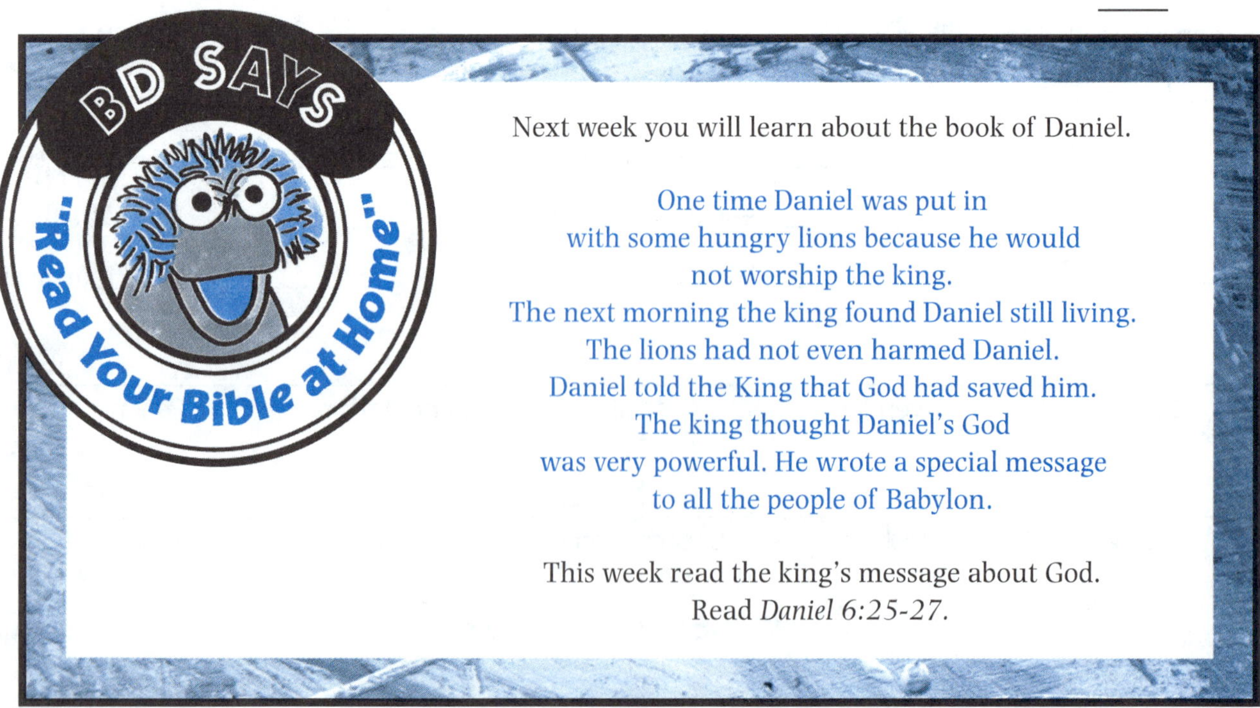

Next week you will learn about the book of Daniel.

One time Daniel was put in with some hungry lions because he would not worship the king. The next morning the king found Daniel still living. The lions had not even harmed Daniel. Daniel told the King that God had saved him. The king thought Daniel's God was very powerful. He wrote a special message to all the people of Babylon.

This week read the king's message about God. Read *Daniel 6:25-27*.

Daniel: A Man Who Dreams ◎ Daniel: A Man Who Dreams ◎ Daniel: A Man Who Dreams

A Psalm of Praise: Psalm 100

Letters and Numbers Scramble

Unscramble the name of each book and print it correctly on the numbered lines.

1. haiasI

___ ___ ___ ___ ___ ___
1 2 3 4 5 6

2. haimereJ

___ ___ ___ ___ ___ ___ ___ ___
7 8 9 10 11 12 13 14

3. smalsP

___ ___ ___ ___ ___ ___
15 16 17 18 19 20

4. snoiLamtatne

___ ___ ___ ___ ___ ___ ___ ___ ___ ___ ___ ___
21 22 23 24 25 26 27 28 29 30 31 32

5. likEeze

___ ___ ___ ___ ___ ___ ___
33 34 35 36 37 38 39

6. verbsPro

___ ___ ___ ___ ___ ___ ___ ___
40 41 42 43 44 45 46 47

7. lanDie

___ ___ ___ ___ ___ ___
48 49 50 51 52 53

Print the matching letters on the numbered lines in this box.

___ ___ ___ ___ ___   ___ ___ ___ ___ ___ ___ ___ ___
11 49 7 30 41   15 9 30 40 6 35 26 32

Making Faces

In the first mirror draw a picture of how you might look when something scares you. In the second mirror draw a picture of how you might look when you realize God is taking care of you.

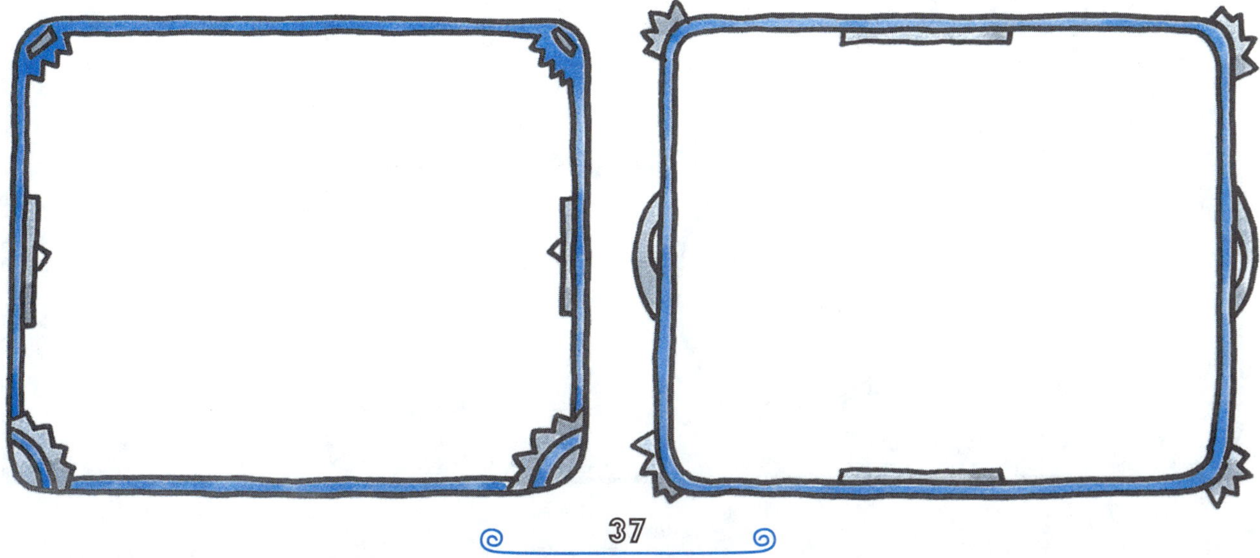

Psalm 100 Acrostic

Print the correct letter on each line from the clue given you.

In pale but not kale ________ and ________ In tell but not sell

In art but not act ________ ________ In hat but not bat

In dare but not dire ________ ________ In far but not fur

In hit but not hat ________ ________ In fan but not fat

In sad but not mad ________ ________ In kit but not hit

In let but not lit ________ ________ In sell but not bell

________ In sag but not sat

________ In fire but not fare

________ In van but not fan

________ In bit but not bat

________ In bin but not bid

________ In flag but not flap

Hosea: Unfaithfulness ◎ Hosea: Unfaithfulness ◎ Hosea: Unfaithfulness ◎ Hosea: Unfaithfulness

Translating the Bible

My Translation

Locate *Isaiah 6:8*. Read the verse. Think about what this verse means to you.
In the space write what the verse means to you. Discuss your answer with a friend in the group.

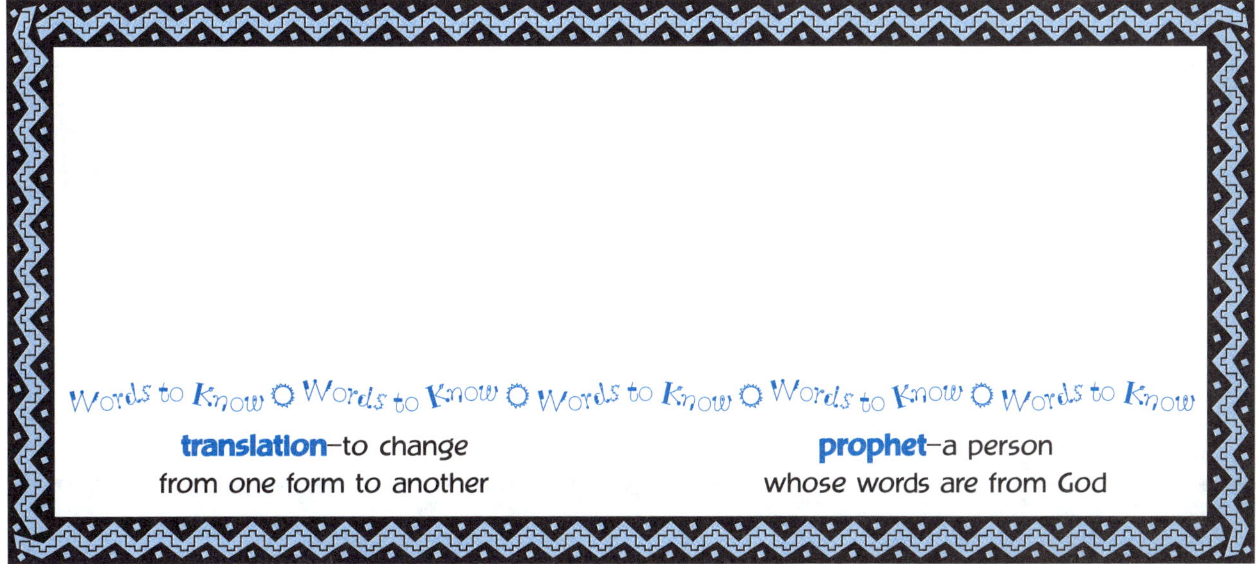

Words to Know ◎ Words to Know ◎ Words to Know ◎ Words to Know ◎ Words to Know

translation–to change from one form to another

prophet–a person whose words are from God

Minor Prophets Wordsearch

Find the Minor Prophet book names and circle (○) them.
Then number the book names in the correct order. Check your answers with your Bible.

Word Box

- Joel
- Jonah
- Amos
- Hosea
- Micah
- Obadiah

J	B	X	R	M	T	S
O	B	A	D	I	A	H
E	C	M	Z	C	G	O
L	J	O	N	A	H	S
K	S	S	J	H	K	E
L	N	P	T	S	Q	A

Back in Time

Find a partner. Read a question, find the correct answer and draw a line to it. Review your answers with your leader. What other facts do you remember about the story?

Questions	Answers
What was the Bible first written on? ◎	◎ Martin Luther
Who translated the Bible into the Latin language? ◎	◎ Jerome
What was invented in 1440 and helped make copies of the Bible more available? ◎	◎ printing press
Who believed that the Bible should be read by everyone, not just church helpers? ◎	◎ scrolls

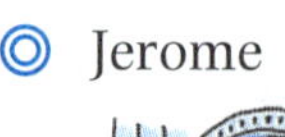

Read *Deuteronomy 4:29* this week.
What does this verse mean to you? This verse is telling you that if you look for the Lord and truly want to find Him, then you will.

Circle (◌) the pictures which help you know about God. List or draw some other ways that you learn about God.

Send Me

Places I Go

Locate and read *Isaiah 6:8* in your Bible. Think about the many different places you go each day. Does God go with you to these places? Do others know that God is with you by the way you act and what you say? Look at the pictures. Circle (○) the places that you go and think about how you can show others that God is with you. Discuss your answers with a friend.

Bible Book Maze

Find your way through the maze to the Bible. Stop as you go and unscramble each of the books of Minor Prophets. Say each of the Bible book names. Say the phrases that you have learned for the first three books.

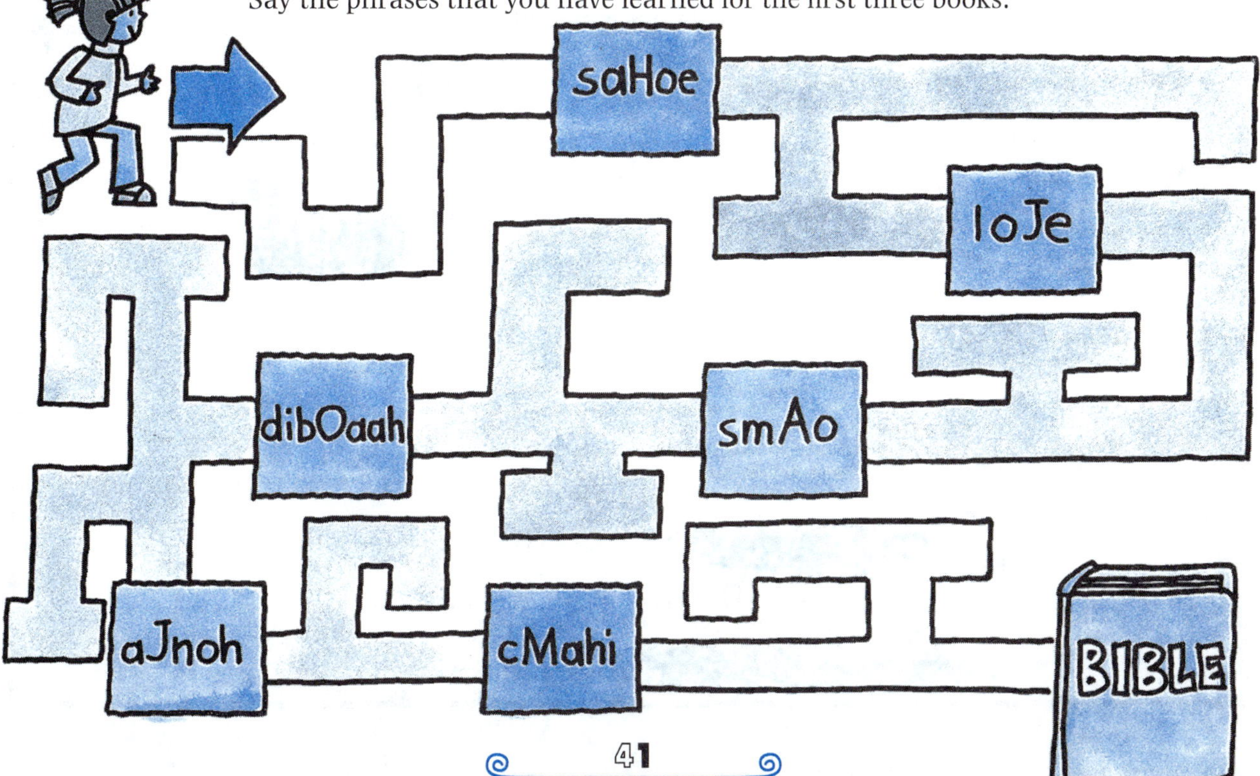

Picture Perfect

Think about the Bible stories that you have learned in Bible Buddies. Which one is your favorite? Why? In the following space, draw a picture of the story you remembered. Show it to a friend. Did you choose the same story? Did you choose a different one?

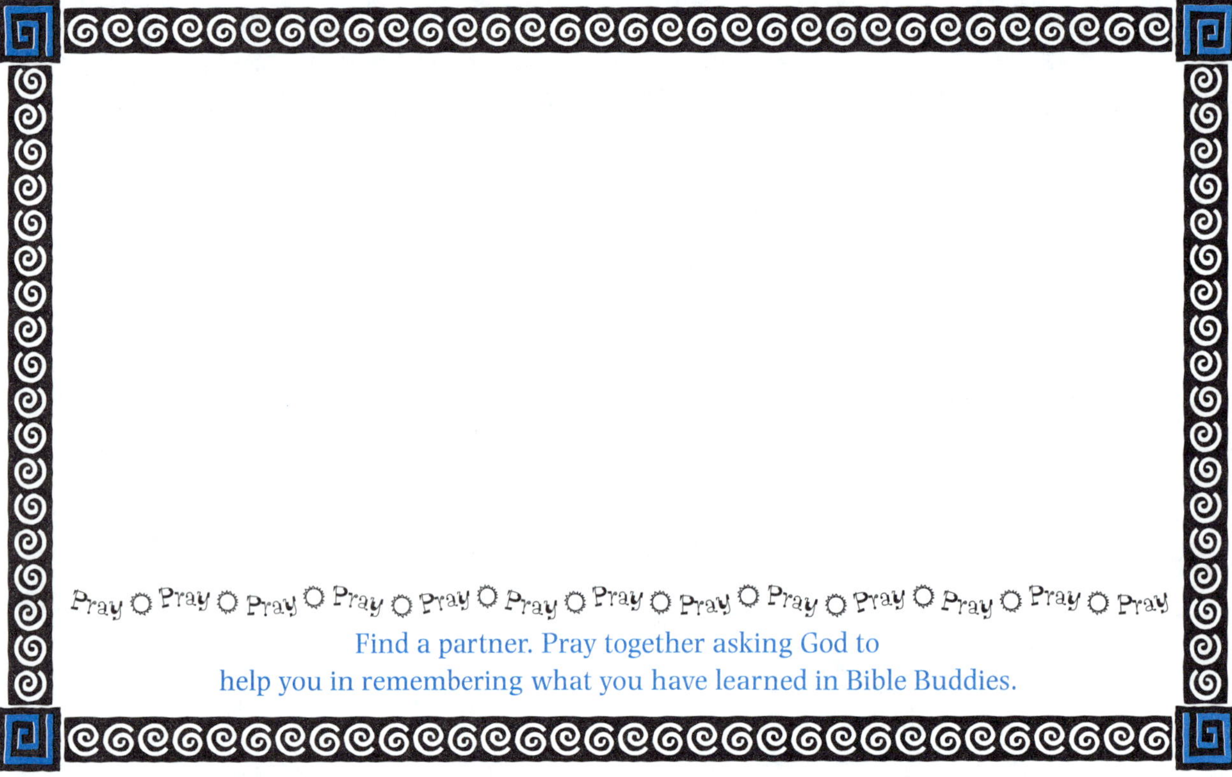

Find a partner. Pray together asking God to help you in remembering what you have learned in Bible Buddies.

BD SAYS

"Read Your Bible at Home"

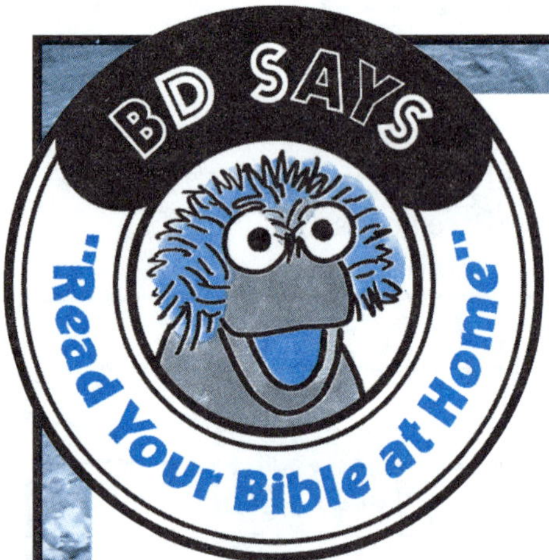

Read *Isaiah 1:2* with a family member this week. How does Isaiah describe the people of Judah? What does it mean to rebel against God? Next week in Bible Buddies you will learn about the ways that the people of Judah rebelled against God.

Read the words in the word box to see how the people of Judah were described. Find the words in the wordsearch. Discuss the word meanings with a parent.

Word Box	
proud	arrogant
evil	sinful
wicked	

B	Z	J	F	P	Q	S	P	G	N	H
G	P	X	M	W	W	I	C	K	E	D
A	R	R	O	G	A	N	T	L	Y	F
C	O	S	W	M	D	F	J	N	S	V
Y	U	K	C	R	Z	U	H	Q	X	L
V	D	R	E	V	I	L	K	T	P	B

Obadiah: Take Care of Your Brother ◎ Obadiah: Take Care of Your Brother ◎ Obadiah: Take Care of Your Brother

Isaiah's Life

A Letter to God

Find a partner. Locate *Isaiah 6:8* in your Bible. Read the Bible verse.
Think about the important messages Isaiah brought to God's people. Think about how important it was for Isaiah to be willing for God to use him for that task.
Think about yourself. How can God use you? How is what you say and do important to Him?
Write a letter to God telling Him of your willingness to do what He wants you to do.

Dear God,

____

____

____

____

____

The Truth about Isaiah's Life

Read the following statements about the Bible story. Decide whether the statement is *true* or *false*. Write a (T) for *true* or (F) for *false* in the space provided. Discuss your answers with your leader.

______ Isaiah was a prophet.

______ Isaiah's ministry lasted 140 years.

______ Isaiah preached to the people of Judah during a time when it ruled over other countries.

______ Isaiah preached often about the holiness of God.

______ Isaiah told about the coming of the Messiah.

______ Isaiah told God's people that God was in control.

Pray

Ask God to be with you everywhere that you go
and remind you that He is in control of everything that happens.

Name that Bible Book

Look at the list of Bible book divisions and Bible books which are listed. Review what you have learned by filling in the blanks with the correct Bible books. Check your answers with a friend. Can you say all the books from memory?

Law

- Genesis
- ____________
- Leviticus
- ____________
- ____________

History

- ____________
- Judges
- ____________
- ____________
- 2 Samuel
- ____________
- 2 Kings
- 1 Chronicles
- ____________
- ____________
- ____________
- ____________

Poetry

- ____________
- ____________
- Proverbs
- Ecclesiastes
- ____________

Major Prophets

- Isaiah
- ____________
- Lamentations
- ____________
- Daniel

Minor Prophets

- ____________
- Joel
- ____________
- Obadiah
- Jonah
- ____________

Locate and read *Isaiah 40:11* this week. Think about what this verse says. What does a shepherd do? Why do you think God is like a shepherd? How are you like a lamb? How can God be like a shepherd to you? Discuss your answers with a family member.

Look at the picture below. Draw a picture of yourself in the shepherd's arms.

Jonah: The People Repent ◎ Micah: A Day in Court ◎ Jonah: The People Repent ◎ Micah: A Day in Court

The Glory of God

Find the Bible Verse

Locate *Isaiah 6:8* in your Bible. Find the hidden words in the picture below from the verse and the word box. After you find all the words, write the whole verse on the space below. Try to write the verse from memory. Say the verse to a friend.

Word Box						
heard	voice	Lord	saying	send	go	me

Isaiah 6:8 ____

Before and After

Look at the names of the Bible books given. In the box above the Bible book, write the name of the book that comes before it. In the box below the Bible book, write the name of the book that comes after it. Check your answers with a leader.

LEVITICUS	1 SAMUEL	ECCLESIASTES	EZEKIEL	OBADIAH

Bible Story Crossword Puzzle

Locate *Isaiah 40* in your Bible. Fill in the blanks to each statement and work the crossword puzzle. Discuss your answers with a friend.

Across

2. The voice in the desert said to prepare the ________________ of the Lord. *(Isaiah 40:3)*

4. The ____________ of the Lord was revealed for people to see. *(Isaiah 40:5)*

5. The Lord takes care of His people like a _________________________. *(Isaiah 40:11)*

Down

1. God is more powerful than all the _________________________. *(Isaiah 40:17)*

3. Isaiah tells God's people to find ___________ from what He says. *(Isaiah 40:1)*

4. ________________ and flowers die, but God's word lasts forever. *(Isaiah 40:8)*

Read *Isaiah 40:28* with a family member this week. What does this verse mean to you? How long does it tell you that God will be here? What is He creator of? This verse says that He will never be tired and that no one can completely understand Him. Can you imagine never getting tired? Hold the following picture in front of a mirror to learn what the Bible Buddies Bible story will be about next week. What does the picture tell you?

The Greatness of God

Nahum: A Flood is Coming ◎ Nahum: A Flood is Coming ◎ Nahum: A Flood is Coming

The Greatness of God

God's Wonders

Locate *Job 37:14* and read the verse. Think about all the things God created. God is great. Draw a picture in the space below of some of your favorite wonders or creations that God made.

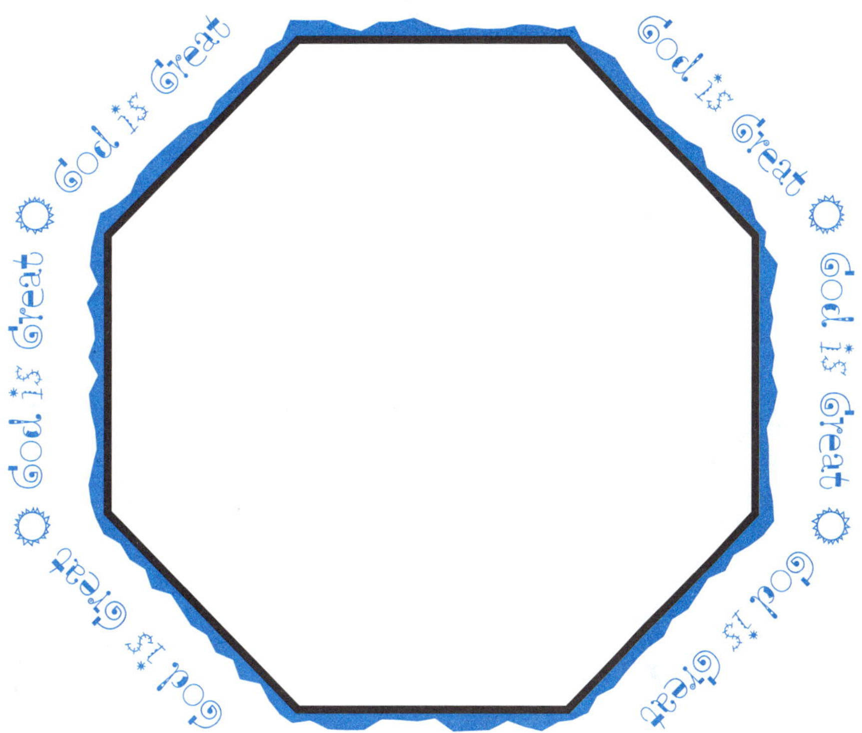

Learning the Books of the Bible

The last six names of the Minor Prophet books are below. Write them in the correct order on the spaces provided. Check your work with your Bible. Can you say the first six books of the Minor Prophets from memory? Practice saying all 12 in order.

Minor Prophet Books

____________________ Zephaniah

____________________ Malachi Nahum

____________________ Zechariah

____________________ Haggai Habakkak

____

____

Match It Up

Look at each of the words or phrases. Locate each Scripture and match up the word or phrase which best describes the verse. How does each word or phrase relate to the Bible story? Discuss your answers with a partner.

Bible Reference

ISAIAH 40:19 ◎   ISAIAH 40:22 ◎   ISAIAH 40:23 ◎   ISAIAH 40:31 ◎

◎ princes and rulers   ◎ wings like eagles   ◎ idols   ◎ grasshoppers

Read *Isaiah 53:3-4* this week. As you read these verses, remember that they are describing Jesus.

At Bible Buddies next week, you will learn why He is sometimes called the suffering servant. Look at the picture of Jesus. Write words from the Bible verses in each space that describe Jesus. Think about what each word means. Remember that Jesus suffered for you. Show your completed picture to a parent. Discuss each word.

The Suffering Servant

My Bible Verse

Read *Job 37:14* in your Bible. You are one of God's wonders.
Write or draw something you like about yourself in the space below.

Learning the Books of the Bible

Match the book of the Bible with its Division.

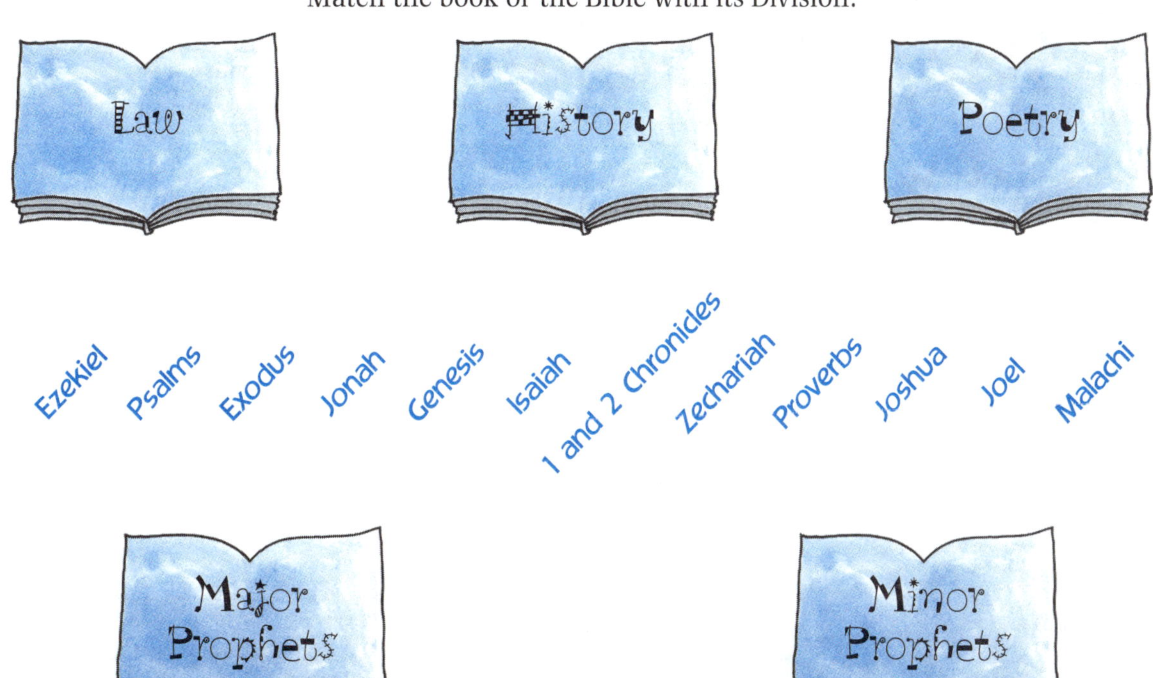

A Journal to God

God wants us to talk to him every day. Habakkuk talked with God by asking Him questions and waiting to hear what God had to say.

Think about something that you would like to ask God or just something you would like to tell God. Write or draw your thoughts in the space below.

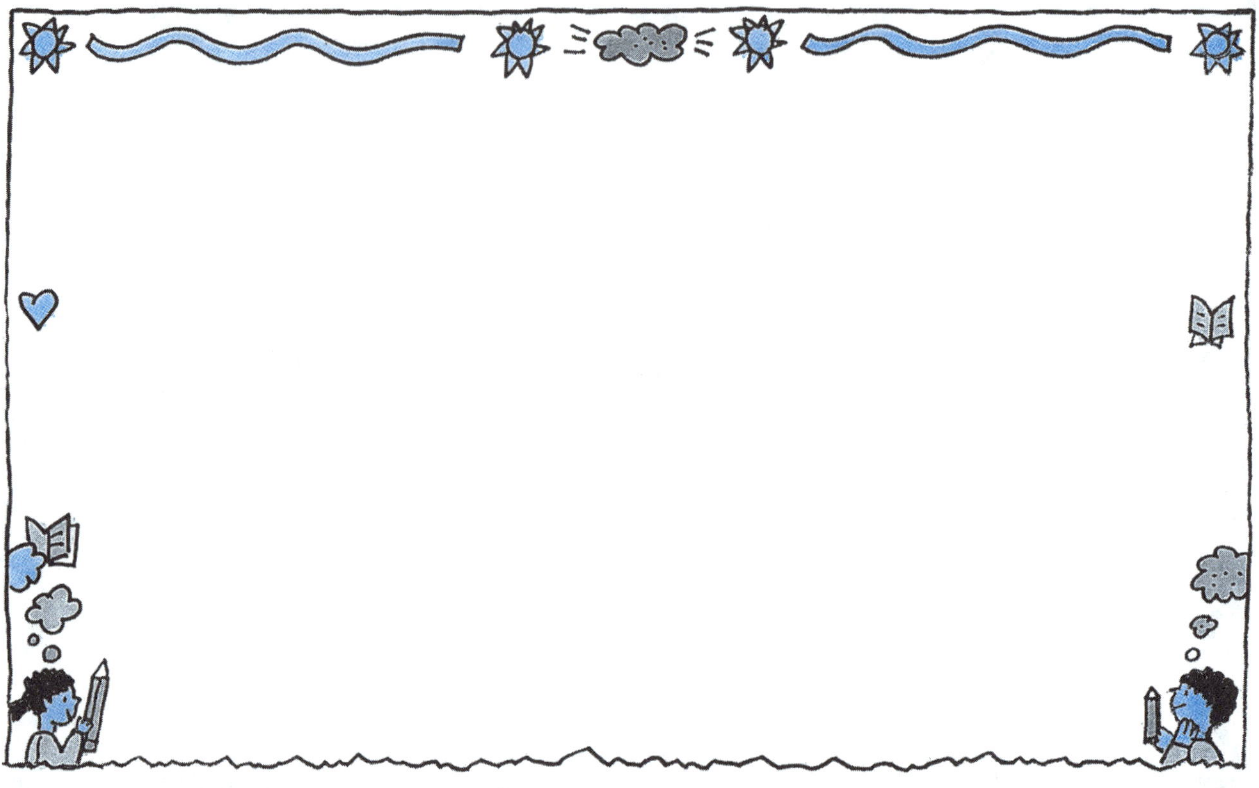

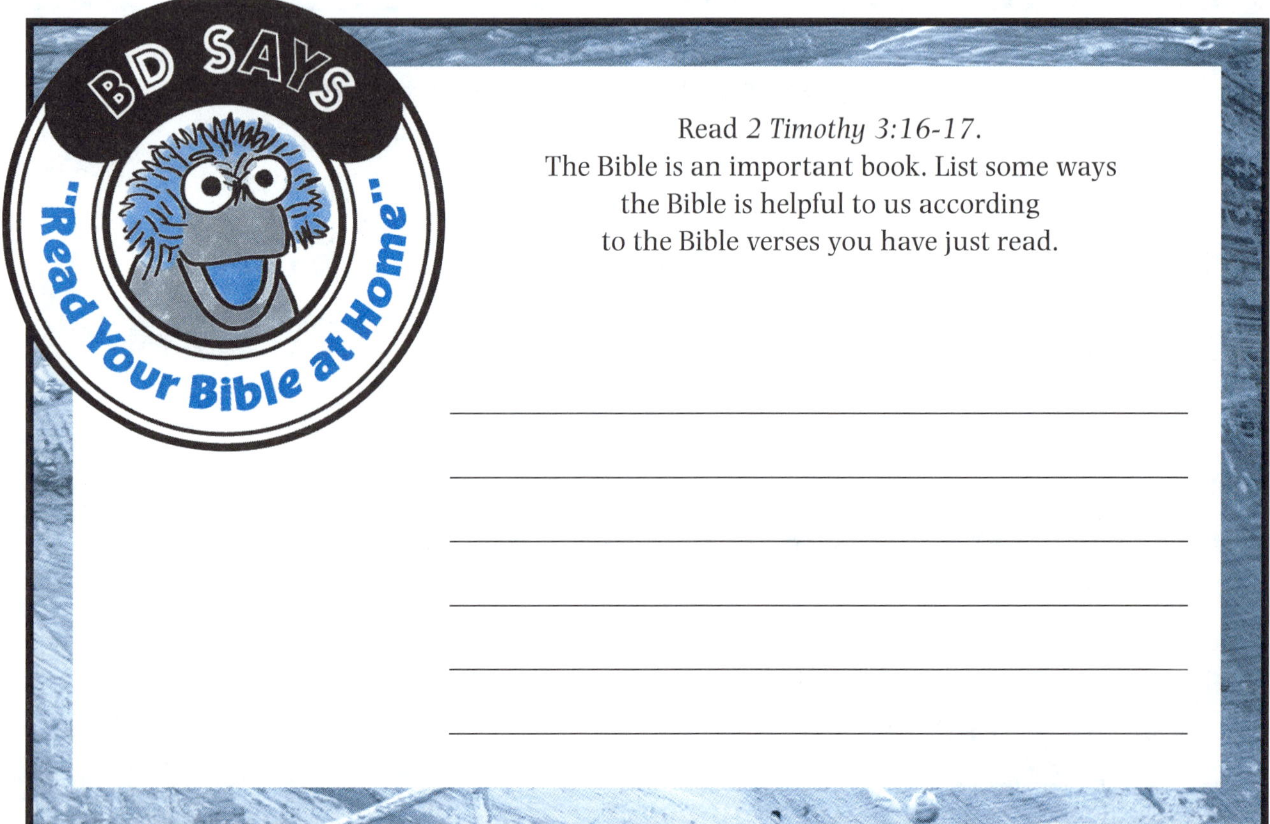

Read *2 Timothy 3:16-17*.
The Bible is an important book. List some ways the Bible is helpful to us according to the Bible verses you have just read.

Zephaniah: The Lord is Coming ◎ Haggai: Finish the Work

Bible History

My Bible Verse

Look up *Job 37:14* in your Bible. Look at the pictures below and circle (○) the things that God has made.

Learning Books of the Bible

In each of the Bibles is a word that is scrambled.
Unscramble the letters in each Bible to spell one of the books of the Minor Prophets.

________________ ________________ ________________

________________ ________________

Picture Code

In the space above the picture, write the first letter of each picture to discover the phrases for Zephaniah and Haggai.

ZEPHANIAH

     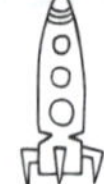 

HAGGAI

      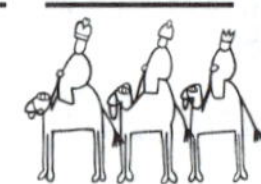

During Bible Buddies we have been learning verses from the Bible. We have studied *Genesis 1:1*, *Numbers 15:39*, *Isaiah 45:5*, *Psalm 56:3*, *Isaiah 6:8*, and *Job 37:14*. Choose one of these as your favorite. Write it in the space below and draw a picture to describe the verse. Put your picture and verse somewhere you will see it to remind you of your special verse.

Game Night

Old Testament Wordsearch

Find the books of the Old Testament. They may be written down or across. One is circled for you. It is Song of Solomon *(Songs)*. Books that have the same name are listed only once. *(For example: 1 and 2 Kings is Kings.)*

Old Testament Old Testament Old Testament

S O N G O F S O L O M O N S O N G S
N C T N U M B E R S T C Z F J O E L
R P X D Z N D E U T E R O N O M Y E
K L A M E N T A T I O N S X S O Z V
J U D G E S N E H E M I A H H B A I
E Z B E X O D U S B R L P S U A M T
R L C N A H U M A L A C H I A D O I
E T M E X I Z E C H A R I A H I S C
M G J S E S T H E R D X J O N A H U
I P M I C A H B S A M U E L R H A S
A J C S K I N G S L J E Z R A W G D
H O S E A A S T P R O V E R B S G A
J B Q M F H A B A K K U K M L Z A N
P S A L M S Z E P H A N I A H K I I
H L K D C H R O N I C L E S V R G E
E C C L E S I A S T E S L P T S N L

Old Testament Old Testament Old Testament

Falling Leaves

Say to a friend the missing words or phrases of the verses on the leaves and match them to the tree (or branch) with the correct Bible reference.

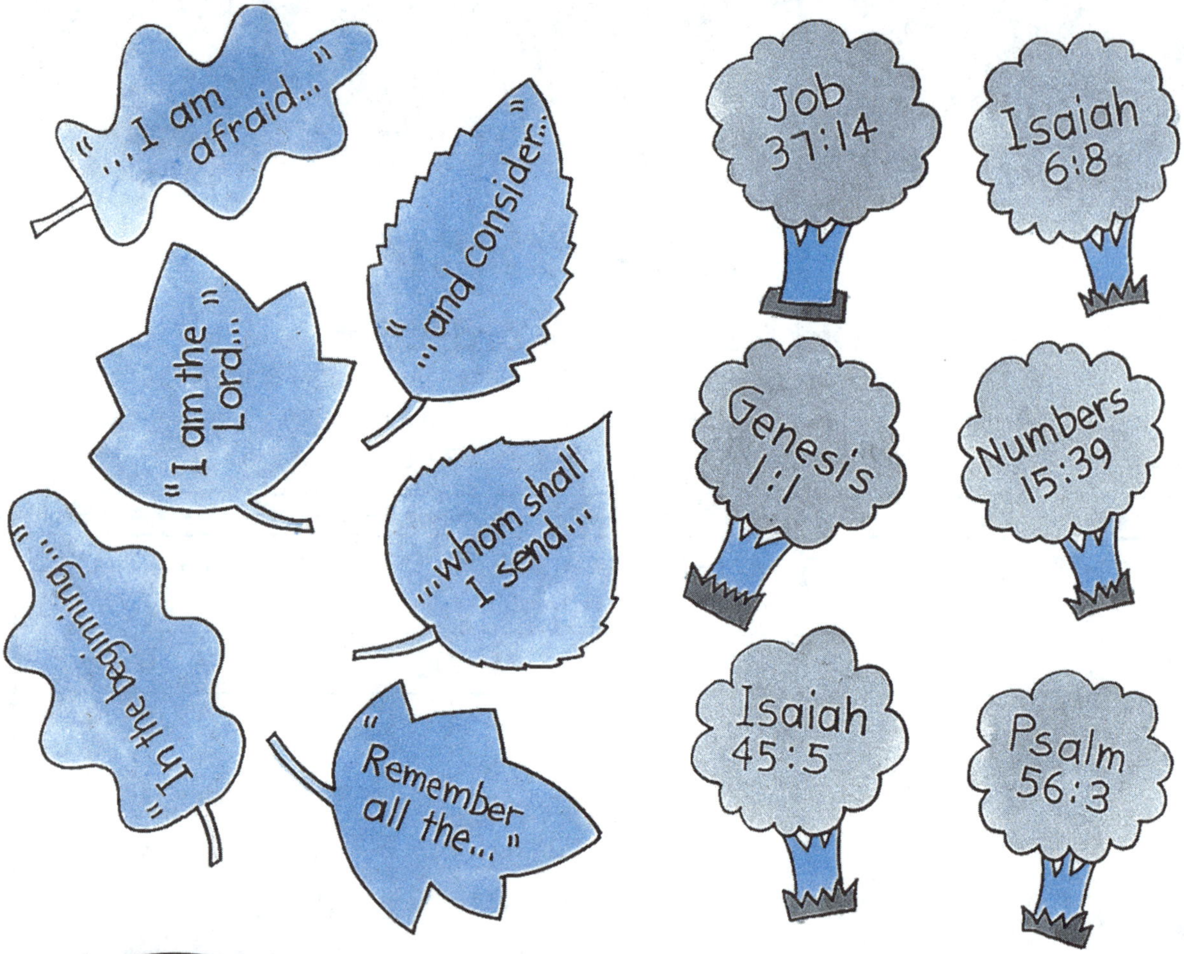

"...I am afraid..."
"...and consider..."
"I am the Lord..."
"...whom shall I send..."
"In the beginning..."
"Remember all the..."
Job 37:14
Isaiah 6:8
Genesis 1:1
Numbers 15:39
Isaiah 45:5
Psalm 56:3

BD SAYS
"Read Your Bible at Home"

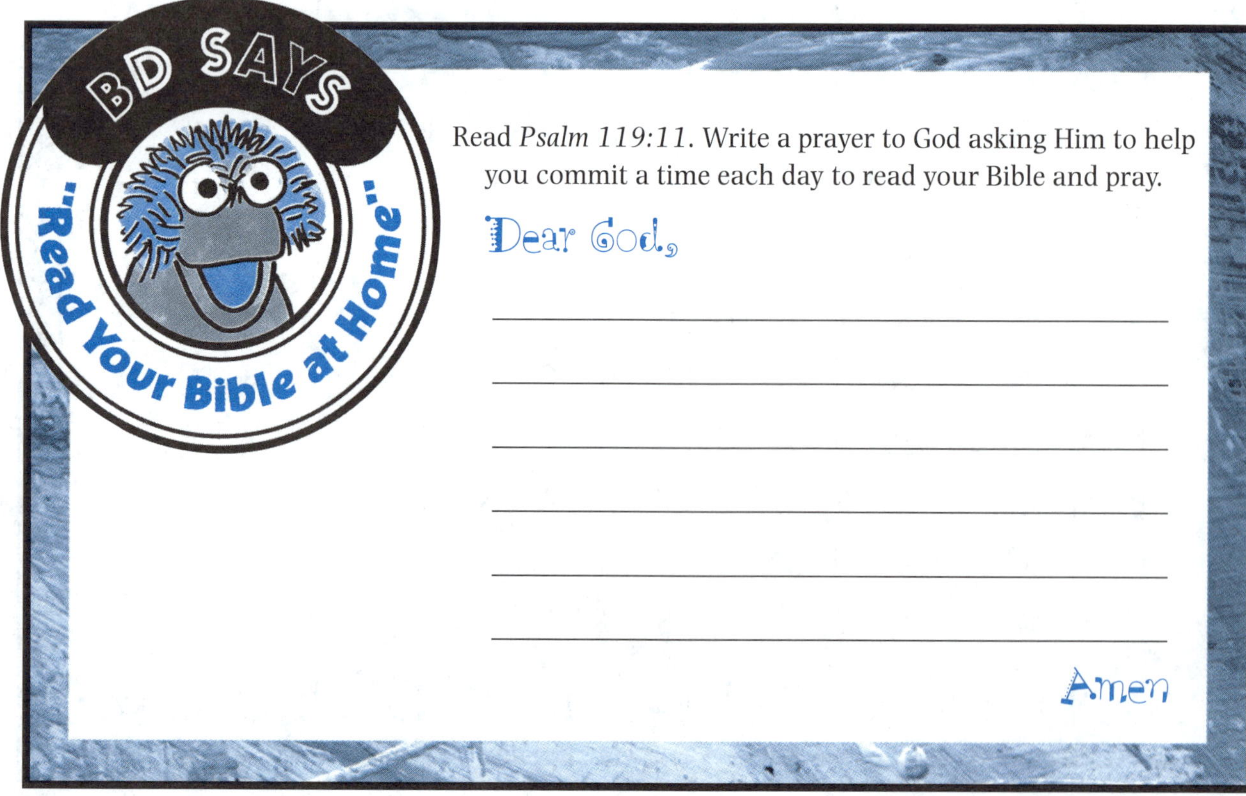

Read *Psalm 119:11*. Write a prayer to God asking Him to help you commit a time each day to read your Bible and pray.

Dear God,

____

____

____

____

____

____

Amen

BIBLE BUDDIES CERTIFICATE
OLD TESTAMENT
Child's Name
has participated in Bible Buddies at
Name of Church
Date
Leaders Name
Leaders Name
BIBLE
B
B
BUDDIES